THE NEW TEMPLE SHAKESPEARE

Edited by M. R. Ridley, M.A.

KING HENRY VI
FIRST PART
by William Shakespeare

London: J. M. DENT & SONS LTD.
New York: E. P. DUTTON & CO. INC.

J. M. DENT & SONS LTD.
Aldine House · Bedford St. · London

Made in Great Britain
by
The Temple Press · Letchworth · Herts

First Published . . 1935
Last Reprinted . . 1948

PRINTED IN GREAT BRITAIN BY
MORRISON AND GIBB LTD., LONDON AND EDINBURGH

Editor's General Note

The Text. The editor has kept before him the aim of presenting to the modern reader the nearest possible approximation to what Shakespeare actually wrote. The text is therefore conservative, and is based on the earliest reliable printed text. But to avoid distraction (*a*) the spelling is modernised, and (*b*) a limited number of universally accepted emendations is admitted without comment. Where a Quarto text exists as well as the First Folio the passages which occur only in the Quarto are enclosed in square brackets [ ] and those which occur only in the Folio in brace brackets { }.

Scene Division. The rapid continuity of the Elizabethan curtainless production is lost by the 'traditional' scene divisions. Where there is an essential difference of place these scene divisions are retained. Where on the other hand the change of place is insignificant the scene division is indicated only by a space on the page. For ease of reference, however, the 'traditional' division is retained at the head of the page and in line numbering.

Notes. Passages on which there are notes are indicated by a † in the margin.

Punctuation adheres more closely than has been usual to the 'Elizabethan' punctuation of the early texts. It is often therefore more indicative of the way in which the lines were to be delivered than of their syntactical construction.

Glossaries are arranged on a somewhat novel principle, not alphabetically, but in the order in which the words or phrases occur. The editor is much indebted to Mr J. N. Bryson for his collaboration in the preparation of the glossaries.

Preface

The Text. The first part of *Henry VI* was printed for the first time, so far as we know, in the First Folio of 1623. In this it differs from the second and third parts, of which (more or less) there are Quartos, and the textual problem with regard to it is to that extent easier. With the exception of a number of unmetrical lines, the text is a good one. The stage-directions are highly elaborate.

Date of Composition. Again there is no evidence except Nashe's allusions to the Talbot scenes, and Henslowe's entry of 'Harey the vj' produced by Strange's men in March 1592, and listed as 'new.' All that this tells us (supposing that the play is our play, and Nashe's remarks on the Talbot scenes are so specific as to leave little doubt) is that Shakespeare had done most of his work on the play, whatever it was, writing it, collaborating in it, or refurbishing another play, by 1592. But it does not necessarily preclude the later addition of a scene or two.

Authorship. But if the textual problem is easy—perhaps indeed fallaciously easy, from the accident that we have only one text—the problem of authorship is as vexatious as it can well be. I propose to say very little about it. The evidence is almost entirely internal, the suggested divisions between various hands are discrepant and agree only in their intricacy, and (many of them) in the dogmatic assurance with which they condemn all other solutions, and with a play of such poor quality I cannot believe that the unravelling of the intricacies is anything but a waste of the ordinary reader's time. If we could reach certainty, or even general agreement, it would be another matter; but it surely is of little importance to arrive at some sort of probability whether the whole play is Shakespeare just beginning to learn his tools, or whether we can get rid of some of it on to Marlowe or Greene or Nashe. Of external evidence there are two pieces; the first is positive, that Heminge and Condell included the play in the canon.[1] The second is negative, that Meres makes no mention of it in his list in 1598; and though the evidence is negative the omission is perhaps a trifle odd, since we know from Henslowe's diary and from an allusion in Nashe[2] that a play of the name, and almost certainly our play, was popular. It is worth while, I think, giving the sections into which Sir Edmund Chambers feels that the play falls:—(a) I. i., iii.; II. v.; III. i., iv.; IV. i., iv.; V. i., iv. (94-end); these are the 'English politics' scenes, and link up with the second and third parts of the play. (b) I. ii., iv.-vi.; II. i.-iii.; III. ii., iii.; IV. vii. (33-end); V. ii., iii. (1-44), iv. (1-93); these are

---

[1] Some critics, notably Alexander (of whose able study I shall have more to say in the Preface to the second and third parts of the play), regard this inclusion as decisive, and consider any doubt of the authorship as involving a charge of dishonesty against Heminge and Condell. This, I think, is to create an unreal, though argumentatively useful, dilemma. It may be pointed out (i) that the case for including the play (to complete the sequence), if there were any reasonable justification, was almost irresistible; (ii) that Heminge and Condell might have other standards for inclusion than those of the modern disintegrating scholar without laying themselves open to a charge of dishonesty; and (iii) that few modern editors would fail to include St Ives, The Ebb Tide, and The Wrecker in the Stevenson canon.

[2] In Pierce Penniless (registered August 8, 1592) Nashe writes: "How would it have joyed brave Talbot (the terror of the French) to think that after he had lyen two hundred yeare in his Toomb, he should triumph againe on the stage, and have his bones new embalmed with the teares of ten thousand spectators at least (at severall times) who, in the Tragedian that represents his person, imagine that they behold him fresh bleeding." And the entries in Henslowe show that the play was at least as popular as such favourites as Hieronimo and the Jew of Malta.

the France-Joan-of-Arc scenes. (c) IV. iii., v., vi., vii. (1-32); these are the Talbot death scenes. (d) V. iii. (45-end), v.; these are the Suffolk-Margaret scenes, and link up with the second and third parts. (e) II. iv.; the Temple garden scene. (f) IV. ii.; a Talbot scene (unrhymed) leading up to (c). Sir Edmund finds Shakespeare's hand unmistakably only in (e) and (f); he is prepared to allow him a share in (a), but certainly not in (b), and thinks that (d) is by a third hand, while (c), often claimed for Shakespeare, he would give to the writer of (b), who may be supposed to have been less bad at rhymed couplets than at blank verse. It is significant that a scholar with so sane a dislike of unnecessary disintegration as Sir Edmund Chambers should yet feel compelled so far to disintegrate this play. One difficulty I feel to be this, that there are some parts which read as certainly Shakespeare's, others as possibly his; that it is hard to suppose that the same man wrote both at the same or even approximately the same time; and that therefore one is perhaps too ready to discard the second class, which one would be ready enough to accept if it were not in the same play as the first. But the problem is one which must be left to the reader himself. At any rate, in many places he will be aware of the dislocating jolt with which one falls or rises from one manner to another. Many of the various views are ably summarised in the Arden edition of the play.

Source. The *Chronicles* of Halle and Holinshed. The latter derived from the former, so that the specific debt is hard to determine. Some details may have been derived from Fabyan.

Duration of Action. There are eight days represented on the stage, with intervals. The historic time is twenty-two years,

from the death of Henry V in 1422 to the marriage alliance of
Henry VI and Margaret in 1444.

Criticism.

Hazlitt.—During the time of the civil wars of York and
Lancaster, England was a perfect bear-garden, and Shakespear
has given us a very lively picture of the scene. The three parts
of *Henry VI* convey a picture of very little else: and are inferior
to the other historical plays. They have brilliant passages: but
the general groundwork is comparatively poor and meagre, the
style ' flat and unraised.'

Dowden.—Among his ' wolfish Earls ' Henry is in constant
terror, not of being himself torn to pieces, but of their flying at one
another's throats. Violent scenes, disturbing the cloistral peace
which it would please him to see reign throughout the universe,
are hateful and terrible to Henry. He rides out hawking with his
Queen and Suffolk, the Cardinal and Gloster; some of the riders
hardly able for an hour to conceal their emulation and their hate.
Henry takes a languid interest in the sport, but all occasions supply
food for his contemplative piety; he suffers from a certain incon-
tinence of devout feeling, and now the falcons set him moralising.
A moment after, and the peers, with Margaret among them, are
bandying furious words. Henry's anguish is extreme, but he hopes
that something may be done by a few moral reflections suitable to
the occasion.

KING HENRY VI

FIRST PART

DRAMATIS PERSONÆ

KING HENRY *the Sixth*.

DUKE OF GLOUCESTER, *uncle to the King, and Protector*.

DUKE OF BEDFORD, *uncle to the King, and Regent of France*.

THOMAS BEAUFORT, *Duke of Exeter, great-uncle to the King*.

HENRY BEAUFORT, *great-uncle to the King, Bishop of Winchester, and afterwards Cardinal*.

JOHN BEAUFORT, *Earl, afterwards Duke, of Somerset*.

RICHARD PLANTAGENET, *son of Richard, late Earl of Cambridge, afterwards Duke of York*.

EARL OF WARWICK. EARL OF SALISBURY. EARL OF SUFFOLK.

LORD TALBOT, *afterwards Earl of Shrewsbury*.

JOHN TALBOT, *his son*.

EDMUND MORTIMER, *Earl of March*.

SIR JOHN FASTOLFE.   SIR WILLIAM GLANSDALE.

SIR WILLIAM LUCY.   SIR THOMAS GARGRAVE.

Mayor of London.

WOODVILE, *Lieutenant of the Tower*.

VERNON, *of the White-Rose or York faction*.

BASSET, *of the Red-Rose or Lancaster faction*.

A Lawyer.   Mortimer's Keepers.

CHARLES, *Dauphin, and afterwards King, of France*.

REIGNIER, *Duke of Anjou, and titular King of Naples*.

DUKE OF BURGUNDY.   BASTARD OF ORLEANS.

DUKE OF ALENÇON.   Governor of Paris.

Master-Gunner of Orleans and his Son.

General of the French forces in Bourdeaux.

A French Sergeant.   A Porter.

An old Shepherd, father to Joan la Pucelle.

MARGARET, *daughter to Reignier, afterwards married to King Henry*.

COUNTESS OF AUVERGNE.

JOAN LA PUCELLE, *commonly called Joan of Arc*.

Lords, Warders of the Tower, Heralds, Officers, Soldiers, Messengers, and Attendants.

Fiends appearing to La Pucelle.

SCENE: *Partly in England, and partly in France*.

THE FIRST PART OF
KING HENRY VI

Act First

Westminster Abbey

Dead March. Enter the Funeral of King Henry the Fifth,
attended on by the Duke of Bedford, Regent of France; the
Duke of Gloucester, Protector; the Duke of Exeter, the
Earl of Warwick, the Bishop of Winchester, Heralds, &c.

Bed. Hung be the heavens with black, yield day to night !
Comets, importing change of times and states,
Brandish your crystal tresses in the sky,
And with them scourge the bad revolting stars
That have consented unto Henry's death !
King Henry the Fifth, too famous to live long !
England ne'er lost a king of so much worth.

Glo. England ne'er had a king until his time.
Virtue he had, deserving to command,
His brandish'd sword did blind men with his beams, 10
His arms spread wider than a dragon's wings,

His sparkling eyes, replete with wrathful fire,
More dazzled and drove back his enemies
Than mid-day sun, fierce bent against their faces.
What should I say? his deeds exceed all speech:
He ne'er lift up his hand but conquered.

Exe. We mourn in black, why mourn we not in blood?
Henry is dead, and never shall revive:
Upon a wooden coffin we attend;
And death's dishonourable victory
We with our stately presence glorify,   20
Like captives bound to a triumphant car.
What? shall we curse the planets of mishap
That plotted thus our glory's overthrow?
Or shall we think the subtle-witted French
Conjurers and sorcerers, that afraid of him
By magic verses have contriv'd his end?

Win. He was a king, bless'd of the King of kings.
Unto the French the dreadful judgement-day
So dreadful will not be as was his sight.   30
The battles of the Lord of hosts he fought:
The church's prayers made him so prosperous.

Glo. The church? where is it? Had not churchmen
    pray'd,
His thread of life had not so soon decay'd:
None do you like but an effeminate prince,

2

Whom, like a school-boy, you may over-awe.

Win. Gloucester, whate'er we like, thou art Protector,
And lookest to command the prince and realm.
Thy wife is proud, she holdeth thee in awe,
More than God or religious churchmen may.   40

Glo. Name not religion, for thou lov'st the flesh,
And ne'er throughout the year to church thou go'st
Except it be to pray against thy foes.

Bed. Cease, cease these jars, and rest your minds in peace :
Let's to the altar : heralds, wait on us :
Instead of gold, we'll offer up our arms,
Since arms avail not now that Henry's dead ;
Posterity, await for wretched years,
When at their mothers' moist eyes babes shall suck,
Our isle be made a nourish of salt tears,   50
And none but women left to wail the dead.
Henry the Fifth, thy ghost I invocate :
Prosper this realm, keep it from civil broils,
Combat with adverse planets in the heavens !
A far more glorious star thy soul will make
Than Julius Cæsar or bright—   †

Enter a Messenger

Mes. My honourable lords, health to you all !
Sad tidings bring I to you out of France,
Of loss, of slaughter, and discomfiture :

3

Guienne, Champagne, Rheims, Orleans, 60
Paris, Guysors, Poictiers, are all quite lost.

Bed. What say'st thou, man, before dead Henry's corse?
Speak softly, or the loss of those great towns
Will make him burst his lead, and rise from death.

Glo. Is Paris lost? is Rouen yielded up?
If Henry were recall'd to life again,
These news would cause him once more yield the
ghost.

Exe. How were they lost? what treachery was us'd?

Mes. No treachery, but want of men and money.
Amongst the soldiers this is muttered, 70
That here you maintain several factions;
And whilst a field should be dispatch'd and fought,
You are disputing of your generals:
One would have lingering wars, with little cost;
Another would fly swift, but wanteth wings;
A third thinks, without expense at all,
By guileful fair words, peace may be obtain'd.
Awake, awake, English nobility!
Let not sloth dim your honours, new-begot:
Cropp'd are the flower-de-luces in your arms; 80
Of England's coat one half is cut away.

Exe. Were our tears wanting to this funeral,
These tidings would call forth their flowing tides.

Bed. Me they concern ; Regent I am of France :
　　Give me my steeled coat, I'll fight for France.
　　Away with these disgraceful wailing robes !
　　Wounds will I lend the French, instead of eyes,
　　To weep their intermissive miseries.

Enter to them another Messenger

Mes. Lords, view these letters, full of bad mischance.
　　France is revolted from the English quite,　　　　90
　　Except some petty towns, of no import :
　　The Dauphin Charles is crowned king in Rheims ;
　　The Bastard of Orleans with him is join'd ;
　　Reignier, Duke of Anjou, doth take his part ;
　　The Duke of Alençon flieth to his side.　　　*Exit*

Exe. The Dauphin crowned king ? all fly to him ?
　　O, whither shall we fly from this reproach ?

Glo. We will not fly, but to our enemies' throats.
　　Bedford, if thou be slack, I'll fight it out.

Bed. Gloucester, why doubt'st thou of my forwardness ?　100
　　An army have I muster'd in my thoughts,
　　Wherewith already France is overrun.

Enter another Messenger

Mes. My gracious lords, to add to your laments,
　　Wherewith you now bedew King Henry's hearse,
　　I must inform you of a dismal fight
　　Betwixt the stout Lord Talbot and the French.

Win. What ? wherein Talbot overcame ? is 't so ?
Mes. O, no ; wherein Lord Talbot was o'erthrown :
    The circumstance I'll tell you more at large.
    The tenth of August last, this dreadful lord,   110
    Retiring from the siege of Orleans,
    Having full scarce six thousand in his troop,
    By three and twenty thousand of the French
    Was round encompassed, and set upon.
    No leisure had he to enrank his men ;
    He wanted pikes to set before his archers ;
    Instead whereof sharp stakes pluck'd out of hedges
    They pitched in the ground confusedly,
    To keep the horsemen off from breaking in.
    More than three hours the fight continued ;   120
    Where valiant Talbot, above human thought,
    Enacted wonders with his sword and lance :
    Hundreds he sent to hell, and none durst stand him ;
    Here, there, and every where, enrag'd he slew :
    The French exclaim'd, the devil was in arms ;
    All the whole army stood agaz'd on him :
    His soldiers spying his undaunted spirit
    A Talbot ! a Talbot ! cried out amain,
    And rush'd into the bowels of the battle.
    Here had the conquest fully been seal'd up,   130
    If Sir John Fastolfe had not play'd the coward :

He, being in the vaward, plac'd behind   †
    With purpose to relieve and follow them,
    Cowardly fled, not having struck one stroke.
    Hence grew the general wreck and massacre ;
    Enclosed were they with their enemies :
    A base Walloon, to win the Dauphin's grace,
    Thrust Talbot with a spear into the back,
    Whom all France, with their chief assembled strength,
    Durst not presume to look once in the face.   140

Bed. Is Talbot slain ? then I will slay myself,
    For living idly here in pomp and ease,
    Whilst such a worthy leader, wanting aid,
    Unto his dastard foemen is betray'd.

Mes. O no, he lives, but is took prisoner,
    And Lord Scales with him, and Lord Hungerford :
    Most of the rest slaughter'd, or took likewise.

Bed. His ransom there is none but I shall pay :
    I 'll hale the Dauphin headlong from his throne,
    His crown shall be the ransom of my friend ;   150
    Four of their lords I 'll change for one of ours.
    Farewell, my masters, to my task will I ;
    Bonfires in France forthwith I am to make,
    To keep our great Saint George's feast withal :
    Ten thousand soldiers with me I will take,
    Whose bloody deeds shall make all Europe quake.

Mes. So you had need, for Orleans is besieged,
 The English army is grown weak and faint:
 The Earl of Salisbury craveth supply,
 And hardly keeps his men from mutiny,   160
 Since they, so few, watch such a multitude.

Exe. Remember, lords, your oaths to Henry sworn;
 Either to quell the Dauphin utterly,
 Or bring him in obedience to your yoke.

Bed. I do remember it, and here take my leave,
 To go about my preparation.   *Exit*

Glo. I 'll to the Tower with all the haste I can,
 To view the artillery and munition,
 And then I will proclaim young Henry king. *Exit*

Exe. To Eltham will I, where the young king is, 170
 Being ordain'd his special governor,
 And for his safety there I 'll best devise. *Exit*

Win. Each hath his place and function to attend:
 I am left out; for me nothing remains.
 But long I will not be Jack out of office;
 The king from Eltham I intend to steal
 And sit at chiefest stern of public weal. *Exeunt*

SCENE II

France.   Before Orleans

*Sound a Flourish.   Enter Charles, Alençon, and Reignier,
marching with Drum and Soldiers*

Cha. Mars his true moving, even as in the heavens
        So in the earth, to this day is not known :
        Late did he shine upon the English side ;
        Now we are victors, upon us he smiles.
        What towns of any moment but we have ?
        At pleasure here we lie, near Orleans ;
        Otherwhiles the famish'd English, like pale ghosts,
        Faintly besiege us one hour in a month.

Al. They want their porridge, and their fat bull-beeves ;
        Either they must be dieted like mules,   10
        And have their provender tied to their mouths,
        Or piteous they will look, like drowned mice.

Rei. Let's raise the siege : why live we idly here ?
        Talbot is taken, whom we wont to fear :
        Remaineth none but mad-brain'd Salisbury,
        And he may well in fretting spend his gall,
        Nor men nor money hath he to make war.

Cha. Sound, sound alarum ! we will rush on them.
        Now for the honour of the forlorn French !

  Him I forgive my death that killeth me   20
  When he sees me go back one foot or fly.   *Exeunt* †
   Here Alarum ; they are beaten back by the English,
       with great loss
    Re-enter Charles, Alençon, and Reignier

Cha. Who ever saw the like ? what men have I ?
  Dogs, cowards, dastards ! I would ne'er have fled,
  But that they left me 'midst my enemies.

Rei. Salisbury is a desperate homicide,
  He fighteth as one weary of his life.
  The other lords, like lions wanting food,
  Do rush upon us as their hungry prey.

Al. Froissart, a countryman of ours, records,
  England all Olivers and Rowlands bred   30
  During the time Edward the Third did reign.
  More truly now may this be verified ;
  For none but Samsons and Goliases
  It sendeth forth to skirmish. One to ten ?
  Lean raw-bon'd rascals, who would e'er suppose ·
  They had such courage and audacity ?

Cha. Let's leave this town, for they are hare-brain'd
   slaves,
  And hunger will enforce them to be more eager :
  Of old I know them ; rather with their teeth
  The walls they 'll tear down than forsake the siege. 40

Rei. I think, by some odd gimmors or device
　　Their arms are set, like clocks, still to strike on ;
　　Else ne'er could they hold out so as they do.
　　By my consent, we 'll even let them alone.

Al. Be it so.

Enter the Bastard of Orleans

Orl. Where 's the Prince Dauphin ? I have news for him.

Cha. Bastard of Orleans, thrice welcome to us.

Orl. Methinks your looks are sad, your cheer appall'd :　　†
　　Hath the late overthrow wrought this offence ?
　　Be not dismay'd, for succour is at hand :　　　　　　　50
　　A holy maid hither with me I bring,
　　Which by a vision sent to her from heaven
　　Ordained is to raise this tedious siege,
　　And drive the English forth the bounds of France.
　　The spirit of deep prophecy she hath,
　　Exceeding the nine sibyls of old Rome :　　　　　　　†
　　What 's past, and what 's to come, she can descry.
　　Speak, shall I call her in ?　Believe my words,
　　For they are certain and unfallible.

Cha. Go, call her in.　(*exit Bastard.*)　But first, to try her
　　　　skill,　　　　　　　　　　　　　　　　　　　60
　　Reignier, stand thou as Dauphin in my place :
　　Question her proudly, let thy looks be stern ;
　　By this means shall we sound what skill she hath.

11

Re-enter the Bastard of Orleans, with Joan La Pucelle

Rei. Fair maid, is 't thou wilt do these wondrous feats ?

Joan. Reignier, is 't thou that thinkest to beguile me ?
Where is the Dauphin ?   Come, come from behind,
I know thee well, though never seen before.
Be not amaz'd, there 's nothing hid from me ;
In private will I talk with thee apart ;
Stand back, you lords, and give us leave awhile.   70

Rei. She takes upon her bravely at first dash.

Joan. Dauphin, I am by birth a shepherd's daughter,
My wit untrain'd in any kind of art :
Heaven and our Lady gracious hath it pleas'd
To shine on my contemptible estate.
Lo, whilst I waited on my tender lambs,
And to sun's parching heat display'd my cheeks,
God's mother deigned to appear to me,
And in a vision full of majesty
Will'd me to leave my base vocation,   80
And free my country from calamity :
Her aid she promis'd and assur'd success :
In complete glory she reveal'd herself ;
And whereas I was black and swart before,
With those clear rays which she infus'd on me
That beauty am I bless'd with which you see.
Ask me what question thou canst possible,

And I will answer unpremeditated :
My courage try by combat, if thou dar'st,
And thou shalt find that I exceed my sex.   90
Resolve on this, thou shalt be fortunate,
If thou receive me for thy warlike mate.

Cha. Thou hast astonish'd me with thy high terms :
Only this proof I'll of thy valour make,
In single combat thou shalt buckle with me ;
And if thou vanquishest, thy words are true,
Otherwise I renounce all confidence.

Joan. I am prepar'd : here is my keen-edg'd sword,
Deck'd with five flower-de-luces on each side,
The which at Touraine, in Saint Katherine's churchyard,
Out of a great deal of old iron I chose forth.   101

Cha. Then come, o' God's name, I fear no woman.

Joan. And while I live, I'll ne'er fly from a man.

Here they fight, and Joan La Pucelle overcomes

Cha. Stay, stay thy hands ! thou art an Amazon,
And fightest with the sword of Deborah.

Joan. Christ's mother helps me, else I were too weak.

Cha. Whoe'er helps thee, 'tis thou that must help me :
Impatiently I burn with thy desire,
My heart and hands thou hast at once subdued.
Excellent Pucelle, if thy name be so,   110
Let me thy servant and not sovereign be :

13

'Tis the French Dauphin sueth to thee thus.

Joan. I must not yield to any rites of love,
  For my profession's sacred from above :
  When I have chased all thy foes from hence,
  Then will I think upon a recompense.

Cha. Meantime look gracious on thy prostrate thrall.

Rei. My lord, methinks, is very long in talk.

Al. Doubtless he shrives this woman to her smock,
  Else ne'er could he so long protract his speech.   120

Rei. Shall we disturb him, since he keeps no mean ?

Al. He may mean more than we poor men do know :
  These women are shrewd tempters with their tongues.

Rei. My lord, where are you ! what devise you on ?
  Shall we give over Orleans, or no ?

Joan. Why, no, I say ; distrustful recreants !
  Fight till the last gasp ; I will be your guard.

Cha. What she says I'll confirm : we'll fight it out.

Joan. Assign'd am I to be the English scourge.
  This night the siege assuredly I'll raise :   130
  Expect Saint Martin's summer, halcyon days,   †
  Since I have entered into these wars.
  Glory is like a circle in the water,
  Which never ceaseth to enlarge itself,
  Till by broad spreading it disperse to nought.
  With Henry's death the English circle ends,

Dispersed are the glories it included :
Now am I like that proud insulting ship
Which Cæsar and his fortune bare at once.   †

Cha. Was Mahomet inspired with a dove ?   140
Thou with an eagle art inspired then.
Helen, the mother of great Constantine,
Nor yet Saint Philip's daughters, were like thee.
Bright star of Venus, fall'n down on the earth,
How may I reverently worship thee enough ?

Al. Leave off delays, and let us raise the siege.

Rei. Woman, do what thou canst to save our honours ;
Drive them from Orleans, and be immortaliz'd.

Cha. Presently we'll try : come, let's away about it :
No prophet will I trust, if she prove false.   *Exeunt* 150

SCENE III

London.   Before the Tower

Enter the Duke of Gloucester, with his Serving-men

Glo. I am come to survey the Tower this day ;
Since Henry's death, I fear there is conveyance.
Where be these warders, that they wait not here ?
Open the gates, 'tis Gloucester that calls.

1.W.(within) Who's there, that knocks so imperiously ?

1. *S.* It is the noble Duke of Gloucester.

2. *W.* (*within*) Whoe'er he be, you may not be let in.

1. *S.* Villains, answer you so the lord protector?

1. *W.* (*within*) The Lord protect him! so we answer him:
    We do no otherwise than we are will'd.   10

Glo. Who willed you? or whose will stands but mine?
    There's none protector of the realm but I.
    Break up the gates, I'll be your warrantize:
    Shall I be flouted thus by dunghill grooms?

        Gloucester's men rush at the Tower Gates, and
            Woodvile the Lieutenant speaks within

Wood. What noise is this? what traitors have we here?

Glo. Lieutenant, is it you whose voice I hear?
    Open the gates, here's Gloucester that would enter.

Wood. Have patience, noble duke, I may not open,
    The Cardinal of Winchester forbids:
    From him I have express commandment   20
    That thou nor none of thine shall be let in.

Glo. Faint-hearted Woodvile, prizest him 'fore me?
    Arrogant Winchester, that haughty prelate,
    Whom Henry, our late sovereign, ne'er could brook?
    Thou art no friend to God, or to the king:
    Open the gates, or I'll shut thee out shortly.

Serving-men. Open the gates unto the lord protector,
    Or we'll burst them open, if that you come not quickly.

Enter to the Protector at the Tower Gates Winchester
and his men in tawny coats

Win. How now, ambitious Humphrey, what means this ?

Glo. Peel'd priest, dost thou command me to be shut out ?   30

Win. I do, thou most usurping proditor,
　　And not protector, of the king or realm.

Glo. Stand back, thou manifest conspirator,
　　Thou that contrivedst to murder our dead lord,
　　Thou that givest whores indulgences to sin,
　　I'll canvass thee in thy broad cardinal's hat,
　　If thou proceed in this thy insolence.

Win. Nay, stand thou back, I will not budge a foot :
　　This be Damascus, be thou cursed Cain,　　　　†
　　To slay thy brother Abel, if thou wilt.　　　　　40

Glo. I will not slay thee, but I'll drive thee back :
　　Thy scarlet robes, as a child's bearing-cloth,
　　I'll use to carry thee out of this place.

Win. Do what thou dar'st ; I beard thee to thy face.

Glo. What ? am I dar'd, and bearded to my face ?
　　Draw, men, for all this privileged place ;
　　Blue coats to tawny coats.   Priest, beware your beard,
　　I mean to tug it, and to cuff you soundly :
　　Under my feet I stamp thy cardinal's hat :
　　In spite of pope, or dignities of church,　　　　50
　　Here by the cheeks I'll drag thee up and down.

17

Win. Gloucester, thou wilt answer this before the pope.

Glo. Winchester goose, I cry, a rope! a rope!
    Now beat them hence, why do you let them stay?
    Thee I'll chase hence, thou wolf in sheep's array.
    Out, tawny coats! out, scarlet hypocrite!

    Here Gloucester's men beat out the Cardinal's men, and enter
      in the hurly-burly the Mayor of London and his Officers

May. Fie, lords! that you, being supreme magistrates,
    Thus contumeliously should break the peace!

Glo. Peace, mayor! thou know'st little of my wrongs:
    Here 's Beaufort, that regards nor God nor king,   60
    Hath here distrain'd the Tower to his use.

Win. Here 's Gloucester, a foe to citizens,
    One that still motions war and never peace,
    O'ercharging your free purses with large fines,
    That seeks to overthrow religion,
    Because he is protector of the realm;
    And would have armour here out of the Tower,
    To crown himself king, and suppress the prince.

Glo. I will not answer thee with words, but blows.

                      Here they skirmish again

May. Nought rests for me in this tumultuous strife   70
    But to make open proclamation:
    Come, officer, as loud as e'er thou canst,
    Cry.

ff. All manner of men assembled here in arms this day,
against God's peace and the king's, we charge and
command you, in his highness' name, to repair to
your several dwelling-places, and not to wear, handle,
or use any sword, weapon, or dagger henceforward,
upon pain of death.

Glo. Cardinal, I 'll be no breaker of the law :   80
But we shall meet, and break our minds at large.

Win. Gloucester, we will meet to thy cost, be sure :
Thy heart-blood I will have for this day's work.

May. I 'll call for clubs, if you will not away.
This cardinal 's more haughty than the devil.

Glo. Mayor, farewell : thou dost but what thou mayst.

Win. Abominable Gloucester, guard thy head,
For I intend to have it ere long.

> *Exeunt, severally, Gloucester and Winchester*
> *with their Serving-men*

May. See the coast clear'd, and then we will depart.
Good God, these nobles should such stomachs bear !   90
I myself fight not once in forty year.   *Exeunt*

SCENE IV

Orleans

Enter, on the walls, a Master Gunner and his Boy

M.G. Sirrah, thou know'st how Orleans is besieg'd,
    And how the English have the suburbs won.
Son. Father, I know, and oft have shot at them,
    Howe'er unfortunate, I miss'd my aim.
M.G. But now thou shalt not.   Be thou rul'd by me:
    Chief master-gunner am I of this town,
    Something I must do to procure me grace.
    The prince's espials have informed me
    How the English, in the suburbs close intrench'd,
    Wont through a secret grate of iron bars 10
    In yonder tower, to overpeer the city,
    And thence discover how with most advantage
    They may vex us with shot or with assault.
    To intercept this inconvenience,
    A piece of ordnance 'gainst it I have plac'd,
    And even these three days have I watch'd,
    If I could see them.
    Now do thou watch, for I can stay no longer.
    If thou spy'st any, run and bring me word,
    And thou shalt find me at the governor's.   *Exit* 20

Son. Father, I warrant you, take you no care,
    I 'll never touble you, if I may spy them.   *Exit*
    Enter, on the turrets, the Lords Salisbury and Talbot, Sir
      William Glansdale, Sir Thomas Gargrave, and others

Sal. Talbot, my life, my joy, again return'd?
    How wert thou handled being prisoner?
    Or by what means got'st thou to be releas'd?
    Discourse, I prithee, on this turret's top.

Tal. The Duke of Bedford had a prisoner,
    Call'd the brave Lord Ponton de Santrailles;
    For him was I exchang'd and ransomed.
    But with a baser man of arms by far   30
    Once in contempt they would have barter'd me:
    Which I disdaining, scorn'd, and craved death,
    Rather than I would be so pill'd esteem'd.   †
    In fine, redeem'd I was as I desir'd.
    But, O! the treacherous Fastolfe wounds my heart,
    Whom with my bare fists I would execute,
    If I now had him brought into my power.

Sal. Yet tell'st thou not how thou wert entertain'd.

Tal. With scoffs and scorns and contumelious taunts.
    In open market-place produc'd they me,   40
    To be a public spectacle to all:
    Here, said they, is the terror of the French,
    The scarecrow that affrights our children so.

Then broke I from the officers that led me,
And with my nails digg'd stones out of the ground,
To hurl at the beholders of my shame:
My grisly countenance made others fly;
None durst come near, for fear of sudden death.
In iron walls they deem'd me not secure;
So great fear of my name 'mongst them was spread,   50
That they suppos'd I could rend bars of steel,
And spurn in pieces posts of adamant:
Wherefore a guard of chosen shot I had,
That walk'd about me every minute while;
And if I did but stir out of my bed,
Ready they were to shoot me to the heart.

Enter the Boy with a linstock

Sal. I grieve to hear what torments you endur'd,
But we will be reveng'd sufficiently.
Now it is supper-time in Orleans:
Here, through this grate, I count each one,   60
And view the Frenchmen how they fortify:
Let us look in, the sight will much delight thee.
Sir Thomas Gargrave, and Sir William Glansdale,
Let me have your express opinions,
Where is best place to make our battery next?

Gar. I think at the north gate, for there stand lords.

Gla. And I here, at the bulwark of the bridge.

22

Tal. For aught I see, this city must be famish'd,
　　Or with light skirmishes enfeebled.
　　　　　　Here they shoot.   Salisbury and Gargrave fall

Sal. O Lord, have mercy on us, wretched sinners !　　70

Gar. O Lord, have mercy on me, woful man !

Tal. What chance is this, that suddenly hath cross'd us ?
　　Speak, Salisbury : at least, if thou canst, speak :
　　How far'st thou, mirror of all martial men ?
　　One of thy eyes and thy cheek's side struck off ?
　　Accursed tower ! accursed fatal hand
　　That hath contriv'd this woful tragedy !
　　In thirteen battles Salisbury o'ercame ;
　　Henry the Fifth he first train'd to the wars ;
　　Whilst any trump did sound, or drum struck up,　　80
　　His sword did ne'er leave striking in the field.
　　Yet liv'st thou, Salisbury ? though thy speech doth fail,
　　One eye thou hast to look to heaven for grace :
　　The sun with one eye vieweth all the world.
　　Heaven, be thou gracious to none alive,
　　If Salisbury wants mercy at thy hands !
　　Bear hence his body, I will help to bury it.
　　Sir Thomas Gargrave, hast thou any life ?
　　Speak unto Talbot, nay, look up to him.
　　Salisbury, cheer thy spirit with this comfort,　　90
　　Thou shalt not die whiles—

23

He beckons with his hand, and smiles on me ;
As who should say, 'When I am dead and gone,
Remember to avenge me on the French.'
Plantagenet, I will ; and like thee, Nero,
Play on the lute, beholding the towns burn :
Wretched shall France be only in my name.

Here an alarum, and it thunders and lightens

What stir is this ? what tumult 's in the heavens ?
Whence cometh this alarum, and the noise ?

Enter a Messenger

Mes. My lord, my lord, the French have gather'd head :   100
The Dauphin, with one Joan la Pucelle join'd,
A holy prophetess, new risen up,
Is come with a great power, to raise the siege.

Here Salisbury lifteth himself up, and groans

Tal. Hear, hear, how dying Salisbury doth groan !
It irks his heart he cannot be reveng'd.
Frenchmen, I'll be a Salisbury to you :
Pucelle or puzzel, dolphin or dogfish,   †
Your hearts I'll stamp out with my horse's heels,
And make a quagmire of your mingled brains.
Convey me Salisbury into his tent,   110
And then we'll try what these dastard Frenchmen
dare.   *Alarum. Exeunt*

SCENE V

The same

Here an alarum again : and Talbot pursueth the Dauphin,
and driveth him : then enter Joan La Pucelle, driving
Englishmen before her, and exit after them : then re-enter
Talbot

Tal. Where is my strength, my valour, and my force ?
Our English troops retire, I cannot stay them,
A woman clad in armour chaseth them.

Re-enter La Pucelle

Here, here she comes.   I 'll have a bout with thee ;
Devil, or devil's dam, I 'll conjure thee :
Blood will I draw on thee, thou art a witch,
And straightway give thy soul to him thou serv'st.

Joan. Come, come, 'tis only I that must disgrace thee.

Here they fight

Tal. Heavens, can you suffer hell so to prevail ?
My breast I 'll burst with straining of my courage,   10
And my from shoulders crack my arms asunder,
But I will chastise this high-minded strumpet.

They fight again

Joan. Talbot, farewell, thy hour is not yet come,

I must go victual Orleans forthwith.

A short alarum : then enter the town
with soldiers

O'ertake me, if thou canst, I scorn thy strength.
Go, go, cheer up thy hungry-starved men,
Help Salisbury to make his testament,
This day is ours, as many more shall be.   *Exit*

Tal. My thoughts are whirled like a potter's wheel,
I know not where I am, nor what I do :   20
A witch, by fear, not force, like Hannibal,
Drives back our troops, and conquers as she lists :
So bees with smoke, and doves with noisome stench,
Are from their hives and houses driven away.
They call'd us, for our fierceness, English dogs ;
Now, like to whelps, we crying run away.

A short alarum

Hark, countrymen, either renew the fight,
Or tear the lions out of England's coat ;
Renounce your soil, give sheep in lions' stead :
Sheep run not half so treacherous from the wolf,
Or horse or oxen from the leopard,   30
As you fly from your oft-subdued slaves.

Alarum.   Here another skirmish

It will not be, retire into your trenches :
You all consented unto Salisbury's death,

For none would strike a stroke in his revenge.
Pucelle is enter'd into Orleans,
In spite of us, or aught that we could do.
O, would I were to die with Salisbury !
The shame hereof will make me hide my head.

Exit Talbot.   Alarum ; retreat ; flourish

SCENE VI

The same

Enter, on the walls, La Pucelle, Charles, Reignier,
Alençon, and Soldiers

Joan. Advance our waving colours on the walls ;
    Rescu'd is Orleans from the English :
    Thus Joan la Pucelle hath perform'd her word.
Cha. Divinest creature, Astræa's daughter,   †
    How shall I honour thee for this success ?
    Thy promises are like Adonis' garden,   †
    That one day bloom'd, and fruitful were the next.
    France, triumph in thy glorious prophetess !
    Recover'd is the town of Orleans :
    More blessed hap did ne'er befall our state.   10
Rei. Why ring not out the bells aloud throughout the
      town ?

Dauphin, command the citizens make bonfires
And feast and banquet in the open streets,
To celebrate the joy that God hath given us.

Al. All France will be replete with mirth and joy,
When they shall hear how we have play'd the men.

Cha. 'Tis Joan, not we, by whom the day is won;
For which, I will divide my crown with her,
And all the priests and friars in my realm
Shall in procession sing her endless praise.   20
A statelier pyramis to her I'll rear
Than Rhodope's or Memphis' ever was;   †
In memory of her, when she is dead,
Her ashes, in an urn more precious
Than the rich-jewel'd coffer of Darius,
Transported shall be at high festivals
Before the kings and queens of France.
No longer on Saint Denis will we cry,
But Joan la Pucelle shall be France's saint.
Come in, and let us banquet royally,   30
After this golden day of victory. *Flourish. Exeunt*

Act Second

SCENE I

Before Orleans

Enter a Sergeant of a band, with two Sentinels

Ser. Sirs, take your places and be vigilant :
 If any noise or soldier you perceive
 Near to the walls, by some apparent sign
 Let us have knowledge at the court of guard.

1.S. Sergeant, you shall. (*exit Sergeant.*) Thus are poor
   servitors
 (When others sleep upon their quiet beds)
 Constrain'd to watch in darkness, rain and cold.

*Enter Talbot, Bedford, Burgundy, and forces, with scaling-
   ladders, their drums beating a dead march*

Tal. Lord Regent, and redoubted Burgundy,
 By whose approach the regions of Artois,
 Wallon, and Picardy, are friends to us,   10
 This happy night the Frenchmen are secure,
 Having all day carous'd and banqueted :
 Embrace we then this opportunity,
 As fitting best to quittance their deceit,

29

Contriv'd by art and baleful sorcery.

Bed. Coward of France, how much he wrongs his fame,
Despairing of his own arm's fortitude,
To join with witches, and the help of hell!

Bur. Traitors have never other company.
But what's that Pucelle whom they term so pure?   20

Tal. A maid, they say.

Bed.   A maid? and be so martial?

Bur. Pray God she prove not masculine ere long,
If underneath the standard of the French
She carry armour as she hath begun.

Tal. Well, let them practise and converse with spirits:
God is our fortress, in whose conquering name
Let us resolve to scale their flinty bulwarks.

Bed. Ascend, brave Talbot, we will follow thee.

Tal. Not all together: better far, I guess,
That we do make our entrance several ways;   30
That if it chance the one of us do fail,
The other yet may rise against their force.

Bed. Agreed: I'll to yond corner.

Bur.   And I to this.

Tal. And here will Talbot mount, or make his grave;
Now, Salisbury, for thee, and for the right
Of English Henry, shall this night appear
How much in duty I am bound to both.

Sen. Arm ! arm ! the enemy doth make assault !

Cry : ' St George,' ' A Talbot '

The French leap over the walls in their shirts. Enter, several
ways, the Bastard of Orleans, Alençon, and Reignier, half
ready, and half unready

Al. How now, my lords ? what, all unready so ?

Orl. Unready ? ay, and glad we 'scap'd so well.   40

Rei. 'Twas time, I trow, to wake and leave our beds,
Hearing alarums at our chamber-doors.

Al. Of all exploits since first I follow'd arms,
Ne'er heard I of a warlike enterprise
More venturous or desperate than this.

Orl. I think this Talbot be a fiend of hell.

Rei. If not of hell, the heavens sure favour him.

Al. Here cometh Charles, I marvel how he sped.

Orl. Tut, holy Joan was his defensive guard.

Enter Charles and La Pucelle

Cha. Is this thy cunning, thou deceitful dame ?   50
Didst thou at first, to flatter us withal,
Make us partakers of a little gain,
That now our loss might be ten times so much ?

Joan. Wherefore is Charles impatient with his friend ?
At all times will you have my power alike ?
Sleeping or waking, must I still prevail,
Or will you blame and lay the fault on me ?

31

Improvident soldiers, had your watch been good,
This sudden mischief never could have fall'n.

Cha. Duke of Alençon, this was your default, 60
That being captain of the watch to-night,
Did look no better to that weighty charge.

Al. Had all your quarters been as safely kept
As that whereof I had the government,
We had not been thus shamefully surprised.

Orl. Mine was secure.

Rei.   And so was mine, my lord.

Cha. And, for myself, most part of all this night,
Within her quarter and mine own precinct
I was employ'd in passing to and fro,
About relieving of the sentinels : 70
Then how, or which way, should they first break in ?

Joan. Question, my lords, no further of the case,
How or which way : 'tis sure they found some place,
But weakly guarded, where the breach was made.
And now there rests no other shift but this,
To gather our soldiers, scatter'd and dispers'd,
And lay new platforms to endamage them.

Alarum. Enter an English Soldier, crying 'A Talbot !
a Talbot !' They fly, leaving their clothes behind

Sol. I 'll be so bold to take what they have left.
The cry of Talbot serves me for a sword,

For I have loaden me with many spoils,   80
Using no other weapon but his name.   *Exit*

SCENE II

Orleans.   Within the town

Enter Talbot, Bedford, Burgundy, a Captain, and others

Bed. The day begins to break, and night is fled,
  Whose pitchy mantle over-veil'd the earth.
  Here sound retreat, and cease our hot pursuit.

                              Retreat sounded

Tal. Bring forth the body of old Salisbury,
  And here advance it in the market-place,
  The middle centre of this cursed town.
  Now have I paid my vow unto his soul;
  For every drop of blood was drawn from him
  There hath at least five Frenchmen died to-night.
  And that hereafter ages may behold   10
  What ruin happen'd in revenge of him,
  Within their chiefest temple I 'll erect
  A tomb, wherein his corpse shall be interr'd:
  Upon the which, that every one may read,
  Shall be engrav'd the sack of Orleans,
  The treacherous manner of his mournful death,

And what a terror he had been to France.
But, lords, in all our bloody massacre,
I muse we met not with the Dauphin's grace,
His new-come champion, virtuous Joan of Arc,   20
Nor any of his false confederates.

Bed. 'Tis thought, Lord Talbot, when the fight began,
Roused on the sudden from their drowsy beds,
They did amongst the troops of armed men
Leap o'er the walls for refuge in the field.

Bur. Myself, as far as I could well discern,
For smoke, and dusky vapours of the night,
Am sure I scar'd the Dauphin and his trull,
When arm in arm they both came swiftly running,
Like to a pair of loving turtle-doves   30
That could not live asunder day or night.
After that things are set in order here,
We'll follow them with all the power we have.

Enter a Messenger

Mes. All hail, my lords ! Which of this princely train
Call ye the warlike Talbot, for his acts
So much applauded through the realm of France ?

Tal. Here is the Talbot, who would speak with him ?

Mes. The virtuous lady, Countess of Auvergne,
With modesty admiring thy renown,
By me entreats, great lord, thou wouldst vouchsafe   40

      To visit her poor castle where she lies,
      That she may boast she hath beheld the man
      Whose glory fills the world with loud report.

Bur. Is it even so ?   Nay, then, I see our wars
      Will turn unto a peaceful comic sport,
      When ladies crave to be encounter'd with.
      You may not, my lord, despise her gentle suit.

Tal. Ne'er trust me then ; for when a world of men
      Could not prevail with all their oratory,
      Yet hath a woman's kindness over-rul'd :   50
      And therefore tell her I return great thanks,
      And in submission will attend on her.
      Will not your honours bear me company ?

Bed. No, truly, it is more than manners will :
      And I have heard it said, unbidden guests
      Are often welcomest when they are gone.

Tal. Well then, alone, since there 's no remedy,
      I mean to prove this lady's courtesy.
      Come hither, captain.   (*whispers*) You perceive **my**
        mind ?

Cap. I do, my lord, and mean accordingly.   *Exeunt* 60

SCENE III

Auvergne.   The Countess's castle

Enter the Countess and her Porter

Cou. Porter, remember what I gave in charge,
    And when you have done so, bring the keys to me.
Por. Madam, I will.   ·   *Exit*
Cou. That plot is laid : if all things fall out right,
    I shall as famous be by this exploit
    As Scythian Tomyris by Cyrus' death.   †
    Great is the rumour of this dreadful knight,
    And his achievements of no less account :
    Fain would mine eyes be witness with mine ears,
    To give their censure of these rare reports.   10

Enter Messenger and Talbot

Mes. Madam,
    According as your ladyship desir'd,
    By message crav'd, so is Lord Talbot come.
Cou. And he is welcome.   What ? is this the man ?
Mes. Madam, it is.
Cou.   Is this the scourge of France ?
    Is this the Talbot, so much fear'd abroad
    That with his name the mothers still their babes ?
    I see report is fabulous and false :

I thought I should have seen some Hercules,
A second Hector, for his grim aspect,   20
And large proportion of his strong-knit limbs.
Alas, this is a child, a silly dwarf !
It cannot be this weak and writhled shrimp
Should strike such terror to his enemies.

Tal. Madam, I have been bold to trouble you ;
But since your ladyship is not at leisure,
I 'll sort some other time to visit you.

Cou. What means he now ?   Go ask him whither he goes.

Mes. Stay, my Lord Talbot, for my lady craves
To know the cause of your abrupt departure.   30

Tal. Marry, for that she 's in a wrong belief,
I go to certify her Talbot 's here.

Re-enter Porter with keys

Cou. If thou be he, then art thou prisoner.

Tal. Prisoner ? to whom ?

Cou.   To me, blood-thirsty lord ;
And for that cause I train'd thee to my house.
Long time thy shadow had been thrall to me,
For in my gallery thy picture hangs :
But now the substance shall endure the like,
And I will chain these legs and arms of thine,
That hast by tyranny these many years   40
Wasted our country, slain our citizens,

And sent our sons and husbands captivate.

Tal. Ha, ha, ha !

Cou. Laughest thou, wretch ? thy mirth shall turn to moan.

Tal. I laugh to see your ladyship so fond
To think that you have aught but Talbot's shadow
Whereon to practice your severity.

Cou. Why ? art not thou the man ?

Tal.   I am indeed.

Cou. Then have I substance too.

Tal. No, no, I am but shadow of myself :
You are deceiv'd, my substance is not here ;
For what you see is but the smallest part
And least proportion of humanity :
I tell you, madam, were the whole frame here,
It is of such a spacious lofty pitch,
Your roof were not sufficient to contain 't.

Cou. This is a riddling merchant for the nonce ;
He will be here, and yet he is not here :
How can these contrarieties agree ?

Tal. That will I show you presently.

                Winds his horn. Drums strike up : a peal
                         of ordnance. Enter Soldiers

How say you, madam ? are you now persuaded
That Talbot is but shadow of himself ?
These are his substance, sinews, arms, and strength,

With which he yoketh your rebellious necks,
Razeth your cities, and subverts your towns
And in a moment makes them desolate.

Cou. Victorious Talbot, pardon my abuse ;
I find thou art no less than fame hath bruited,
And more than may be gather'd by thy shape.
Let my presumption not provoke thy wrath,   70
For I am sorry that with reverence
I did not entertain thee as thou art.

Tal. Be not dismay'd, fair lady, nor misconster
The mind of Talbot, as you did mistake
The outward composition of his body.
What you have done hath not offended me ;
Nor other satisfaction do I crave,
But only, with your patience, that we may
Taste of your wine, and see what cates you have,
For soldiers' stomachs always serve them well.   80

Cou. With all my heart, and think me honoured,
To feast so great a warrior in my house.   *Exeunt*

SCENE IV

London.   The Temple-garden

*Enter the Earls of Somerset, Suffolk, and Warwick ;
Richard Plantagenet, Vernon, and another Lawyer*

Pla. Great lords and gentlemen, what means this silence ?
    Dare no man answer in a case of truth ?

Suf. Within the Temple-hall we were too loud ;
    The garden here is more convenient.

Pla. Then say at once if I maintain'd the truth ;
    Or else was wrangling Somerset in the error ?

Suf. Faith, I have been a truant in the law,
    And never yet could frame my will to it ;
    And therefore frame the law unto my will.

Som. Judge you, my lord of Warwick, then, between us.   10

War. Between two hawks, which flies the higher pitch,
    Between two dogs, which hath the deeper mouth,
    Between two blades, which bears the better temper,
    Between two horses, which doth bear him best,
    Between two girls, which hath the merriest eye,
    I have perhaps some shallow spirit of judgement :
    But in these nice sharp quillets of the law,
    Good faith, I am no wiser than a daw.

Pla. Tut, tut, here is a mannerly forbearance :

The truth appears so naked on my side,   20
That any purblind eye may find it out.

Som. And on my side it is so well apparell'd,
So clear, so shining and so evident
That it will glimmer through a blind man's eye.

Pla. Since you are tongue-tied, and so loath to speak,
In dumb significants proclaim your thoughts :
Let him that is a true-born gentleman,
And stands upon the honour of his birth,
If he suppose that I have pleaded truth,
From off this brier pluck a white rose with me.   30

Som. Let him that is no coward nor no flatterer,
But dare maintain the party of the truth,
Pluck a red rose from off this thorn with me.

War. I love no colours ; and without all colour
Of base insinuating flattery
I pluck this white rose with Plantagenet.

Suf. I pluck this red rose, with young Somerset,
And say withal, I think he held the right.

Ver. Stay, lords and gentlemen, and pluck no more,
Till you conclude that he, upon whose side   40
The fewest roses are cropp'd from the tree,
Shall yield the other in the right opinion.

Som. Good Master Vernon, it is well objected :
If I have fewest, I subscribe in silence.

Pla. And I.

Ver. Then for the truth and plainness of the case,
    I pluck this pale and maiden blossom here,
    Giving my verdict on the white rose side.

Som. Prick not your finger as you pluck it off,
    Lest bleeding you do paint the white rose red,   50
    And fall on my side so against your will.

Ver. If I, my lord, for my opinion bleed,
    Opinion shall be surgeon to my hurt,
    And keep me on the side where still I am.

Som. Well, well, come on, who else?

Law. Unless my study and my books be false,
    The argument you held was wrong in you;

                          To Somerset

    In sign whereof, I pluck a white rose too.

Pla. Now, Somerset, where is your argument?

Som. Here in my scabbard, meditating that   60
    Shall dye your white rose in a bloody red.

Pla. Meantime your cheeks do counterfeit our roses,
    For pale they look with fear, as witnessing
    The truth on our side.

Som.   No, Plantagenet;
    'Tis not for fear, but anger, that thy cheeks
    Blush for pure shame, to counterfeit our roses,
    And yet thy tongue will not confess thy error.

Pla. Hath not thy rose a canker, Somerset ?

Som. Hath not thy rose a thorn, Plantagenet ?

Pla. Ay, sharp and piercing, to maintain his truth,   70
    Whiles thy consuming canker eats his falsehood.

Som. Well, I 'll find friends to wear my bleeding roses,
    That shall maintain what I have said is true,
    Where false Plantagenet dare not be seen.

Pla. Now, by this maiden blossom in my hand,
    I scorn thee and thy fashion, peevish boy.

Suf. Turn not thy scorns this way, Plantagenet.

Pla. Proud Pole, I will, and scorn both him and thee.

Suf. I 'll turn my part thereof into thy throat.

Som. Away, away, good William de la Pole !   80
    We grace the yeoman by conversing with him.

War. Now, by God's will, thou wrong'st him, Somerset ;
    His grandfather was Lionel Duke of Clarence,
    Third son to the third Edward King of England :
    Spring crestless yeomen from so deep a root ?

Pla. He bears him on the place's privilege,
    Or durst not for his craven heart say thus.

Som. By him that made me, I 'll maintain my words
    On any plot of ground in Christendom.
    Was not thy father, Richard, Earl of Cambridge,   90
    For treason executed in our late king's days ?
    And by his treason stand'st not thou attainted

43

> Corrupted, and exempt from ancient gentry?
> His trespass yet lives guilty in thy blood,
> And, till thou be restor'd, thou art a yeoman.

Pla. My father was attached, not attainted,
Condemn'd to die for treason, but no traitor;
And that I 'll prove on better men than Somerset,
Were growing time once ripen'd to my will.
For your partaker Pole and you yourself,   100
I 'll note you in my book of memory,
To scourge you for this apprehension:
Look to it well and say you are well warn'd.

Som. Ah, thou shalt find us ready for thee still;
And know us by these colours for thy foes,
For these my friends in spite of thee shall wear.

Pla. And, by my soul, this pale and angry rose,
As cognizance of my blood-drinking hate,
Will I for ever and my faction wear,
Until it wither with me to my grave,   110
Or flourish to the height of my degree.

Suf. Go forward, and be chok'd with thy ambition!
And so farewell, until I meet thee next.   *Exit*

Som. Have with thee, Pole. Farewell, ambitious Richard.
                                               Exit

Pla. How I am brav'd and must perforce endure it!

War. This blot that they object against your house

44

Shall be wip'd out in the next parliament   †
Call'd for the truce of Winchester and Gloucester;
And if thou be not then created York,
I will not live to be accounted Warwick.   120
Meantime, in signal of my love to thee,
Against proud Somerset and William Pole,
Will I upon thy party wear this rose:
And here I prophesy: this brawl to-day,
Grown to this faction in the Temple-garden,
Shall send between the red rose and the white
A thousand souls to death and deadly night.

Pla. Good Master Vernon, I am bound to you,
That you on my behalf would pluck a flower.

Ver. In your behalf still will I wear the same.   130

Law. And so will I.

Pla. Thanks, gentle sir.
Come, let us four to dinner: I dare say
This quarrel will drink blood another day.   *Exeunt*

SCENE V

The Tower of London

Enter Mortimer, brought in a chair, and Gaolers

Mor. Kind keepers of my weak decaying age,
Let dying Mortimer here rest himself.

Even like a man new haled from the rack,
So fare my limbs with long imprisonment;
And these grey locks, the pursuivants of death,
Nestor-like aged, in an age of care,
Argue the end of Edmund Mortimer.
These eyes, like lamps whose wasting oil is spent,
Wax dim, as drawing to their exigent;
Weak shoulders, overborne with burthening grief,   10
And pithless arms, like to a wither'd vine
That droops his sapless branches to the ground:
Yet are these feet, whose strengthless stay is numb,
Unable to support this lump of clay,
Swift-winged with desire to get a grave,
As witting I no other comfort have.
But tell me, keeper, will my nephew come?

1.*G.* Richard Plantagenet, my lord, will come:
We sent unto the Temple, unto his chamber;
And answer was return'd, that he will come.   20

Mor. Enough: my soul shall then be satisfied.
Poor gentleman! his wrong doth equal mine.
Since Henry Monmouth first began to reign,
Before whose glory I was great in arms,
This loathsome sequestration have I had;
And even since then hath Richard been obscur'd,
Depriv'd of honour and inheritance.

46

But now the arbitrator of despairs,
Just death, kind umpire of men's miseries,
With sweet enlargement doth dismiss me hence :   30
I would his troubles likewise were expir'd,
That so he might recover what was lost.

Enter Richard Plantagenet

1.*G.* My lord, your loving nephew now is come.

Mor. Richard Plantagenet, my friend, is he come ?

Pla. Ay, noble uncle, thus ignobly us'd,
Your nephew, late despised Richard, comes.

Mor. Direct mine arms I may embrace his neck,
And in his bosom spend my latter gasp :
O, tell me when my lips do touch his cheeks,
That I may kindly give one fainting kiss.   40
And now declare, sweet stem from York's great stock,
Why didst thou say of late thou wert despis'd ?

Pla. First, lean thine aged back against mine arm,
And, in that ease, I 'll tell thee my disease.
This day, in argument upon a case,
Some words there grew 'twixt Somerset and me ;
Among which terms he us'd his lavish tongue
And did upbraid me with my father's death :
Which obloquy set bars before my tongue,
Else with the like I had requited him.   50
Therefore good uncle, for my father's sake,

In honour of a true Plantagenet,
And for alliance sake, declare the cause
My father, Earl of Cambridge, lost his head.

Mor. That cause, fair nephew, that imprison'd me,
And hath detain'd me all my flowering youth
Within a loathsome dungeon, there to pine,
Was cursed instrument of his decease.

Pla. Discover more at large what cause that was,
For I am ignorant and cannot guess.   60

Mor. I will, if that my fading breath permit,
And death approach not ere my tale be done.
Henry the Fourth, grandfather to this king,
Depos'd his nephew Richard, Edward's son,
The first-begotten and the lawful heir
Of Edward king, the third of that descent:
During whose reign the Percies of the north,
Finding his usurpation most unjust,
Endeavour'd my advancement to the throne:
The reason mov'd these warlike lords to this   70
Was, for that—young King Richard thus remov'd,
Leaving no heir begotten of his body—
I was the next by birth and parentage;
For by my mother I derived am
From Lionel Duke of Clarence, the third son
To King Edward the Third; whereas he

From John of Gaunt doth bring his pedigree,
Being but fourth of that heroic line.
But mark : as in this haughty great attempt
They laboured to plant the rightful heir,   80
I lost my liberty, and they their lives.
Long after this, when Henry the Fifth,
Succeeding his father Bolingbroke, did reign,
Thy father, Earl of Cambridge, then deriv'd
From famous Edmund Langley, Duke of York,
Marrying my sister, that thy mother was,
Again, in pity of my hard distress,
Levied an army, weening to redeem
And have install'd me in the diadem :
But, as the rest, so fell that noble earl   90
And was beheaded.   Thus the Mortimers,
In whom the title rested, were suppress'd.

Pla. Of which, my lord, your honour is the last.

Mor. True ; and thou seest that I no issue have,
And that my fainting words do warrant death :
Thou art my heir ; the rest I wish thee gather :
But yet be wary in thy studious care.

Pla. Thy grave admonishments prevail with me :
But yet, methinks, my father's execution
Was nothing less than bloody tyranny.   100

Mor. With silence, nephew, be thou politic :

49

Strong-fixed is the house of Lancaster,
And like a mountain, not to be remov'd.
But now thy uncle is removing hence;
As princes do their courts, when they are cloy'd
With long continuance in a settled place.

Pla. O, uncle, would some part of my young years
Might but redeem the passage of your age!

Mor. Thou dost then wrong me, as that slaughterer doth
Which giveth many wounds, when one will kill.   110
Mourn not, except thou sorrow for my good;
Only give order for my funeral:
And so farewell, and fair be all thy hopes,
And prosperous be thy life in peace and war!   *Dies*

Pla. And peace, no war, befall thy parting soul!
In prison hast thou spent a pilgrimage,
And like a hermit overpass'd thy days.
Well, I will lock his counsel in my breast,
And what I do imagine, let that rest.
Keepers, convey him hence, and I myself   120
Will see his burial better than his life.

    Exeunt Gaolers, bearing out the body of Mortimer
Here dies the dusky torch of Mortimer,
Chok'd with ambition of the meaner sort,
And for those wrongs, those bitter injuries,
Which Somerset hath offer'd to my house,

I doubt not but with honour to redress ;
And therefore haste I to the parliament,
Either to be restored to my blood,
Or make my ill the advantage of my good.   *Exit*

Act Third

SCENE I

London.   The Parliament-house

Flourish.   Enter King, Exeter, Gloucester, Warwick, Somerset, and Suffolk ; the Bishop of Winchester, Richard Plantagenet, and others.   Gloucester offers to put up a bill ; Winchester snatches it, tears it

Win. Com'st thou with deep premeditated lines ?
With written pamphlets studiously devis'd,
Humphrey of Gloucester ?   If thou canst accuse,
Or aught intend'st to lay unto my charge,
Do it without invention, suddenly,
As I with sudden and extemporal speech
Purpose to answer what thou canst object.

Glo. Presumptuous priest, this place commands my patience,
Or thou shouldst find thou hast dishonour'd me.

Think not, although in writing I preferr'd   10
The manner of thy vile outrageous crimes,
That therefore I have forg'd, or am not able
Verbatim to rehearse the method of my pen:
No, prelate, such is thy audacious wickedness,
Thy lewd, pestiferous, and dissentious pranks,
As very infants prattle of thy pride.
Thou art a most pernicious usurer,
Froward by nature, enemy to peace,
Lascivious, wanton, more than well beseems
A man of thy profession and degree;   20
And for thy treachery, what's more manifest?
In that thou laid'st a trap to take my life,
As well at London-bridge as at the Tower.
Beside, I fear me, if thy thoughts were sifted,
The king, thy sovereign, is not quite exempt
From envious malice of thy swelling heart.
*Win.*Gloucester, I do defy thee. Lords, vouchsafe
To give me hearing what I shall reply.
If I were covetous, ambitious, or perverse,
As he will have me, how am I so poor?   30
Or how haps it I seek not to advance
Or raise myself, but keep my wonted calling?
And for dissension, who preferreth peace
More than I do?—except I be provok'd.

No, my good lords, it is not that offends,
It is not that that hath incens'd the duke:
It is because no one should sway but he,
No one but he should be about the king;
And that engenders thunder in his breast,
And makes him roar these accusations forth.   40
But he shall know I am as good—

Glo.   As good?
Thou bastard of my grandfather!

Win. Ay, lordly sir; for what are you, I pray,
But one imperious in another's throne?

Glo. Am I not protector, saucy priest?

Win. And am not I a prelate of the church?

Glo. Yes, as an outlaw in a castle keeps,
And useth it to patronage his theft.

Win. Unreverent Gloster!

Glo.   Thou art reverent,
Touching thy spiritual function, not thy life.   50

Win. Rome shall remedy this.

War.   Roam thither, then.

Som. My lord, it were your duty to forbear.

War. Ay, see the bishop be not overborne.

Som. Methinks my lord should be religious,
And know the office that belongs to such.

War. Methinks his lordship should be humbler;

It fitteth not a prelate so to plead.

Som. Yes, when his holy state is touch'd so near.

War. State holy or unhallow'd, what of that?
Is not his grace protector to the king? 6c

Pla. (*aside*) Plantagenet, I see, must hold his tongue,
Lest it be said 'Speak, sirrah, when you should;
Must your bold verdict enter talk with lords?' †
Else would I have a fling at Winchester.

King. Uncles of Gloucester, and of Winchester,
The special watchmen of our English weal,
I would prevail, if prayers might prevail,
To join your hearts in love and amity.
O, what a scandal is it to our crown,
That two such noble peers as ye should jar! 7c
Believe me, lords, my tender years can tell
Civil dissension is a viperous worm,
That gnaws the bowels of the commonwealth.

A noise within, 'Down with the tawny-coats!'
What tumult's this?

War.　　　　　　　An uproar, I dare warrant,
Begun through malice of the bishop's men.

A noise again, 'Stones! stones!'
Enter Mayor

May. O, my good lords, and virtuous Henry,
Pity the city of London, pity us!

54

The bishop and the Duke of Gloucester's men,
Forbidden late to carry any weapon,
Have fill'd their pockets full of pebble stones,   80
And banding themselves in contrary parts
Do pelt so fast at one another's pate
That many have their giddy brains knock'd out :
Our windows are broke down in every street,
And we for fear compell'd to shut our shops.

Enter Serving-men, in skirmish, with bloody pates

King. We charge you, on allegiance to ourself,
To hold your slaughtering hands, and keep the peace.
Pray, uncle Gloucester, mitigate this strife.

1.S. Nay, if we be forbidden stones, we 'll fall to it with
our teeth.   90

2.S. Do what ye dare, we are as resolute.   *Skirmish again*

Glo. You of my household, leave this peevish broil
And set this unaccustom'd fight aside.

3.S. My lord, we know your grace to be a man
Just, and upright ; and, for your royal birth,
Inferior to none but to his majesty :
And ere that we will suffer such a prince,
So kind a father of the commonweal,
To be disgraced by an inkhorn mate,
We and our wives and children all will fight,   100
And have our bodies slaughter'd by thy foes.

1.*S.* Ay, and the very parings of our nails
    Shall pitch a field when we are dead.   *Begin again*

Glo.   Stay, stay, I say!
    And if you love me, as you say you do,
    Let me persuade you to forbear awhile.

King. O, how this discord doth afflict my soul!
    Can you, my Lord of Winchester, behold
    My sighs and tears, and will not once relent?
    Who should be pitiful, if you be not?
    Or who should study to prefer a peace,   110
    If holy churchmen take delight in broils?

War. Yield, my lord protector, yield, Winchester,
    Except you mean with obstinate repulse
    To slay your sovereign, and destroy the realm.
    You see what mischief, and what murder too,
    Hath been enacted through your enmity;
    Then be at peace, except ye thirst for blood.

Win. He shall submit, or I will never yield.

Glo. Compassion on the king commands me stoop,
    Or I would see his heart out, ere the priest   120
    Should ever get that privilege of me.

War. Behold, my Lord of Winchester, the duke
    Hath banish'd moody discontented fury,
    As by his smoothed brows it doth appear:
    Why look you still so stern, and tragical?

Glo. Here, Winchester, I offer thee my hand.

King. Fie, uncle Beaufort! I have heard you preach
  That malice was a great and grievous sin;
  And will not you maintain the thing you teach,
  But prove a chief offender in the same?   130

War. Sweet king! the bishop hath a kindly gird.
  For shame, my lord of Winchester, relent!
  What, shall a child instruct you what to do?

Win. Well, Duke of Gloucester, I will yield to thee   †
  Love for thy love, and hand for hand I give.

Glo. (*aside*) Ay, but I fear me with a hollow heart.—
  See here, my friends and loving countrymen,
  This token serveth for a flag of truce
  Betwixt ourselves and all our followers:
  So help me God, as I dissemble not!   140

Win. (*aside*) So help me God, as I intend it not!

King. O loving uncle, kind Duke of Gloucester,
  How joyful am I made by this contract!
  Away, my masters, trouble us no more,
  But join in friendship, as your lords have done.

1.S. Content, I'll to the surgeon's.

2.S.   And so will I.

3.S. And I will see what physic the tavern affords.

              Exeunt Serving-men, Mayor, &c.

War. Accept this scroll, most gracious sovereign,

57

Which in the right of Richard Plantagenet
We do exhibit to your majesty.   150

Glo. Well urg'd, my Lord of Warwick: for, sweet prince,
An if your grace mark every circumstance,
You have great reason to do Richard right;
Especially for those occasions
At Eltham place I told your majesty.

King. And those occasions, uncle, were of force:
Therefore, my loving lords, our pleasure is
That Richard be restored to his blood.

War. Let Richard be restored to his blood,
So shall his father's wrongs be recompens'd.   160

Win. As will the rest, so willeth Winchester.

King. If Richard will be true, not that alone
But all the whole inheritance I give
That doth belong unto the house of York,
From whence you spring by lineal descent.

Pla. Thy humble servant vows obedience,
And humble service, till the point of death.

King. Stoop then, and set your knee against my foot,
And in reguerdon of that duty done,
I gird thee with the valiant sword of York: 170
Rise, Richard, like a true Plantagenet,
And rise created princely Duke of York.

Pla. And so thrive Richard as thy foes may fall,

And as my duty springs, so perish they
That grudge one thought against your majesty !

All. Welcome, high prince, the mighty Duke of York !

Som. (aside) Perish, base prince, ignoble Duke of York !

Glo. Now will it best avail your majesty
To cross the seas, and to be crown'd in France :
The presence of a king engenders love   180
Amongst his subjects and his loyal friends,
As it disanimates his enemies.

King. When Gloucester says the word, King Henry goes,
For friendly counsel cuts off many foes.

Glo. Your ships already are in readiness.

Sennet. Flourish. Exeunt all but Exeter

Exe. Ay, we may march in England, or in France,
Not seeing what is likely to ensue.
This late dissension grown betwixt the peers
Burns under feigned ashes of forg'd love,
And will at last break out into a flame :   190
As fester'd members rot but by degree,
Till bones and flesh and sinews fall away,
So will this base and envious discord breed.
And now I fear that fatal prophecy
Which in the time of Henry nam'd the fifth
Was in the mouth of every sucking babe,
That Henry born at Monmouth should win all,

And Henry born at Windsor lose all :
Which is so plain, that Exeter doth wish
His days may finish ere that hapless time.   *Exit* 200

SCENE II

France.   Before Rouen

*Enter La Pucelle disguised, with four Soldiers with sacks
upon their backs*

Joan. These are the City gates, the gates of Rouen,
Through which our policy must make a breach :
Take heed, be wary how you place your words,
Talk like the vulgar sort of market men,
That come to gather money for their corn.
If we have entrance, as I hope we shall,
And that we find the slothful watch but weak,
I 'll by a sign give notice to our friends,
That Charles the Dauphin may encounter them.

1.S. Our sacks shall be a mean to sack the city,   10
And we be lords and rulers over Rouen ;
Therefore we 'll knock.   *Knocks*

Watch. (*within*) Qui est là ?

Joan. Paysans, pauvres gens de France ;
Poor market folks that come to sell their corn.

60

Watch. Enter, go in, the market bell is rung.

Joan. Now, Rouen, I'll shake thy bulwarks to the ground.

                                                   Exeunt

     Enter Charles, the Bastard of Orleans, Alençon,
                Reignier, and forces

Cha. Saint Denis bless this happy stratagem,
     And once again we'll sleep secure in Rouen.

Orl. Here enter'd Pucelle and her practisants ;   20
     Now she is there, how will she specify,
     ' Here is the best and safest passage in ' ?

Rei. By thrusting out a torch from yonder tower ;
     Which, once discern'd, shows that her meaning is,
     No way to that, for weakness, which she enter'd.
     Enter La Pucelle on the top, thrusting out a torch burning

Joan. Behold, this is the happy wedding torch
     That joineth Rouen unto her countrymen,
     But burning fatal to the Talbotites !   *Exit*

Orl. See, noble Charles, the beacon of our friend,
     The burning torch in yonder turret stands.   30

Cha. Now shine it like a comet of revenge,
     A prophet to the fall of all our foes !

Rei. Defer no time, delays have dangerous ends ;
     Enter, and cry ' The Dauphin ! ' presently,
     And then do execution on the watch.

                               Alarum.   Exeunt

An alarum. Enter Talbot in an excursion

Tal. France, thou shalt rue this treason with thy tears,
    If Talbot but survive thy treachery.
    Pucelle, that witch, that damned sorceress,
    Hath wrought this hellish mischief unawares,
    That hardly we escap'd the pride of France.   *Exit*   **40**

An alarum : excursions. Bedford, brought in sick in a chair.
   Enter Talbot and Burgundy without : within La Pucelle,
   Charles, Bastard, Alençon, and Reignier, on the walls

Joan. Good morrow, gallants, want ye corn for bread ?
    I think the Duke of Burgundy will fast
    Before he'll buy again at such a rate :
    'Twas full of darnel ; do you like the taste ?
Bur. Scoff on, vile fiend and shameless courtezan !
    I trust ere long to choke thee with thine own,
    And make thee curse the harvest of that corn.
Cha. Your grace may starve, perhaps, before that time.
Bed. O, let no words, but deeds, revenge this treason !
Joan. What will you do, good grey-beard ? break a lance,   **50**
    And run a tilt at death within a chair ?
Tal. Foul fiend of France, and hag of all despite,
    Encompass'd with thy lustful paramours,
    Becomes it thee to taunt his valiant age,
    And twit with cowardice a man half dead ?

Damsel, I'll have a bout with you again,
Or else let Talbot perish with this shame.

Joan. Are ye so hot, sir ? yet, Pucelle, hold thy peace ;
If Talbot do but thunder, rain will follow.

The English whisper together in council

God speed the parliament ! who shall be the speaker ? 60

Tal. Dare ye come forth and meet us in the field ?

Joan. Belike your lordship takes us then for fools,
To try if that our own be ours or no.

Tal. I speak not to that railing Hecate,
But unto thee, Alençon, and the rest ;
Will ye, like soldiers, come and fight it out ?

Al. Signior, no.

Tal. Signior, hang ! base muleters of France !
Like peasant foot-boys do they keep the walls,
And dare not take up arms like gentlemen. 70

Joan. Away, captains ! let's get us from the walls,
For Talbot means no goodness by his looks.
God b'uy, my lord ! we came but to tell you
That we are here.   *Exeunt from the walls*

Tal. And there will we be too, ere it be long,
Or else reproach be Talbot's greatest fame !
Vow, Burgundy, by honour of thy house,
Prick'd on by public wrongs sustain'd in France,
Either to get the town again, or die :

63

And I, as sure as English Henry lives,   80
And as his father here was conqueror,
As sure as in this late-betrayed town
Great Cœur-de-lion's heart was buried,
So sure I swear to get the town, or die.

Bur. My vows are equal partners with thy vows.

Tal. But, ere we go, regard this dying prince,
The valiant Duke of Bedford.   Come, my lord,
We will bestow you in some better place,
Fitter for sickness and for crazy age.

Bed. Lord Talbot, do not so dishonour me :   90
Here will I sit, before the walls of Rouen
And will be partner of your weal or woe.

Bur. Courageous Bedford, let us now persuade you.

Bed. Not to be gone from hence ; for once I read
That stout Pendragon, in his litter sick,   †
Came to the field, and vanquished his foes :
Methinks I should revive the soldiers' hearts,
Because I ever found them as myself.

Tal. Undaunted spirit in a dying breast !
Then be it so : heavens keep old Bedford safe !   100
And now no more ado, brave Burgundy,
But gather we our forces out of hand,
And set upon our boasting enemy.

Exeunt all but Bedford and Attendants

An alarum : excursions.   Enter Sir John Fastolfe
and a Captain

Cap. Whither away, Sir John Fastolfe, in such haste ?

Fas. Whither away ? to save myself by flight :
 We are like to have the overthrow again.

Cap. What ? will you fly, and leave Lord Talbot ?

Fas.   Ay,
 All the Talbots in the world, to save my life.   *Exit*

Cap. Cowardly knight, ill fortune follow thee !   *Exit*
      Retreat : excursions.   La Pucelle, Alençon, and
                  Charles fly

Bed. Now, quiet soul, depart when heaven please,   110
 For I have seen our enemies' overthrow.
 What is the trust or strength of foolish man ?
 They that of late were daring with their scoffs
 Are glad and fain by flight to save themselves.
      Bedford dies, and is carried in by two in his chair
      An alarum.   Re-enter Talbot, Burgundy, and the rest

Tal. Lost, and recover'd in a day again !
 This is a double honour, Burgundy :
 Yet heavens have glory for this victory !

Bur. Warlike and martial Talbot, Burgundy
 Enshrines thee in his heart and there erects
 Thy noble deeds as valour's monuments.   120

Tal. Thanks, gentle duke.   But where is Pucelle now ?

I think her old familiar is asleep :
Now where 's the Bastard's braves, and Charles his
    gleeks ?
What, all amort ?   Rouen hangs her head for grief
That such a valiant company are fled.
Now will we take some order in the town,
Placing therein some expert officers,
And then depart to Paris to the king,
For there young Henry with his nobles lie.

Bur. What wills Lord Talbot pleaseth Burgundy.   **130**

Tal. But yet, before we go, let 's not forget
The noble Duke of Bedford late deceas'd,
But see his exequies fulfill'd in Rouen :
A braver soldier never couched lance,
A gentler heart did never sway in court ;
But kings and mightiest potentates must die,
For that 's the end of human misery.   *Exeunt*

SCENE III

The plains near Rouen

*Enter Charles, the Bastard of Orleans, Alençon,
La Pucelle, and forces*

Joan. Dismay not, princes, at this accident,
Nor grieve that Rouen is so recovered :

Care is no cure, but rather corrosive,
For things that are not to be remedied.
Let frantic Talbot triumph for a while,
And like a peacock sweep along his tail;
We 'll pull his plumes, and take away his train,
If Dauphin and the rest will be but rul'd.

Cha. We have been guided by thee hitherto,
And of thy cunning had no diffidence;   10
One sudden foil shall never breed distrust.

Orl. Search out thy wit for secret policies,
And we will make thee famous through the world.

Al. We 'll set thy statue in some holy place,
And have thee reverenc'd like a blessed saint:
Employ thee then, sweet virgin, for our good.

Joan. Then thus it must be, this doth Joan devise:
By fair persuasions, mix'd with sugar'd words,
We will entice the Duke of Burgundy
To leave the Talbot, and to follow us.   20

Cha. Ay, marry, sweeting, if we could do that,
France were no place for Henry's warriors,
Nor should that nation boast it so with us,
But be extirped from our provinces.

Al. For ever should they be expuls'd from France,
And not have title of an earldom here.

Joan. Your honours shall perceive how I will work,

67

To bring this matter to the wished end.

Drum sounds afar off

Hark ! by the sound of drum you may perceive
Their powers are marching unto Paris-ward. 30

*Here sound an English march.   Enter, and pass over
at a distance, Talbot and his forces*

There goes the Talbot, with his colours spread,
And all the troops of English after him.

French march.   Enter the Duke of Burgundy and forces

Now in the rearward comes the duke and his :
Fortune in favour makes him lag behind.
Summon a parley, we will talk with him.

Trumpets sound a parley

Cha. A parley with the Duke of Burgundy !

Bur. Who craves a parley with the Burgundy ?

Joan. The princely Charles of France, thy countryman.

Bur. What say'st thou, Charles ? for I am marching hence.

Cha. Speak, Pucelle, and enchant him with thy words. 40

Joan. Brave Burgundy, undoubted hope of France,
     Stay, let thy humble handmaid speak to thee.

Bur. Speak on, but be not over-tedious.

Joan. Look on thy country, look on fertile France,
     And see the cities and the towns defac'd
     By wasting ruin of the cruel foe.
     As looks the mother on her lowly babe,

When death doth close his tender-dying eyes,
See, see the pining malady of France ;
Behold the wounds, the most unnatural wounds,   50
Which thou thyself hast given her woful breast.
O, turn thy edged sword another way ;
Strike those that hurt, and hurt not those that help.
One drop of blood drawn from thy country's bosom
Should grieve thee more than streams of foreign gore :
Return thee therefore with a flood of tears,
And wash away thy country's stained spots.

Bur. Either she hath bewitch'd me with her words,
Or nature makes me suddenly relent.

Joan. Besides, all French and France exclaims on thee,   60
Doubting thy birth and lawful progeny.
Who join'st thou with, but with a lordly nation
That will not trust thee but for profit's sake ?
When Talbot hath set footing once in France,
And fashion'd thee that instrument of ill,
Who then but English Henry will be lord,
And thou be thrust out, like a fugitive ?
Call we to mind, and mark but this for proof ;
Was not the Duke of Orleans thy foe ?
And was he not in England prisoner ?   70
But when they heard he was thine enemy,
They set him free without his ransom paid,

In spite of Burgundy and all his friends.
See then, thou fight'st against thy countrymen,
And join'st with them will be thy slaughter-men.
Come, come, return; return, thou wandering lord,
Charles and the rest will take thee in their arms.

Bur. I am vanquished; these haughty words of hers
Have batter'd me like roaring cannon-shot,
And made me almost yield upon my knees.   80
Forgive me, country, and sweet countrymen,
And, lords, accept this hearty kind embrace:
My forces and my power of men are yours:
So farewell, Talbot, I 'll no longer trust thee.

Joan. (*aside*) Done like a Frenchman: turn and turn again!

Cha. Welcome, brave duke! thy friendship makes us fresh.

Orl. And doth beget new courage in our breasts.

Al. Pucelle hath bravely play'd her part in this,
And doth deserve a coronet of gold.

Cha. Now let us on, my lords, and join our powers,   90
And seek how we may prejudice the foe.   *Exeunt*

SCENE IV

Paris. The palace

Enter the King, Gloucester, Bishop of Winchester, York, Suffolk,
Somerset, Warwick, Exeter : Vernon, Basset, and others.
To them with his Soldiers, Talbot

Tal. My gracious prince, and honourable peers,
Hearing of your arrival in this realm,
I have awhile given truce unto my wars,
To do my duty to my sovereign :
In sign whereof, this arm, that hath reclaim'd
To your obedience fifty fortresses,
Twelve cities, and seven walled towns of strength,
Beside five hundred prisoners of esteem,
Lets fall his sword before your highness' feet,
And with submissive loyalty of heart   10
Ascribes the glory of his conquest got
First to my God, and next unto your grace.   *Kneels*

King. Is this the Lord Talbot, uncle Gloucester,
That hath so long been resident in France ?

Glo. Yes, if it please your majesty, my liege.

King. Welcome, brave captain and victorious lord !
When I was young (as yet I am not old)
I do remember how my father said

A stouter champion never handled sword.
Long since we were resolved of your truth,   20
Your faithful service, and your toil in war ;
Yet never have you tasted our reward,
Or been reguerdon'd with so much as thanks,
Because till now we never saw your face :
Therefore, stand up, and, for these good deserts,
We here create you Earl of Shrewsbury ;
And in our coronation take your place.

    Sennet. Flourish. Exeunt all but Vernon and Basset

Ver. Now, sir, to you, that were so hot at sea,
Disgracing of these colours that I wear
In honour of my noble Lord of York :—   30
Dar'st thou maintain the former words thou spak'st ?

Bas. Yes, sir, as well as you dare patronage
The envious barking of your saucy tongue
Against my lord the Duke of Somerset.

Ver. Sirrah, thy lord, I honour as he is.

Bas. Why, what is he ? as good a man as York.

Ver. Hark ye ; not so : in witness, take ye that.

                        Strikes him

Bas. Villain, thou know'st the law of arms is such
That whoso draws a sword, 'tis present death,
Or else this blow should broach thy dearest blood.   40
But I 'll unto his majesty, and crave

I may have liberty to venge this wrong;
When thou shalt see I 'll meet thee to thy cost.

Ver. Well, miscreant, I 'll be there as soon as you,
And after meet you, sooner than you would.   *Exeunt*

Act Fourth

SCENE I

Paris.   A hall of state

*Enter the King, Gloucester, Bishop of Winchester, York, Suffolk,
Somerset, Warwick, Talbot, Exeter, the Governor of
Paris, and others*

Glo. Lord bishop, set the crown upon his head.

Win. God save King Henry, of that name the sixth!

Glo. Now, governor of Paris, take your oath,
That you elect no other king but him;
Esteem none friends but such as are his friends,
And none your foes but such as shall pretend
Malicious practices against his state:
This shall ye do, so help you righteous God!
                    Enter Sir John Fastolfe

Fas. My gracious sovereign, as I rode from Calais,

To haste unto your coronation,   10
A letter was deliver'd to my hands,
Writ to your grace, from the Duke of Burgundy.

Tal. Shame to the Duke of Burgundy, and thee !
I vow'd, base knight, when I did meet thee next,
To tear the garter from thy craven's leg,

                              Plucking it off

Which I have done, because unworthily
Thou wast installed in that high degree.
Pardon me, princely Henry, and the rest :
This dastard, at the battle of Patay,
When but in all I was six thousand strong,   20
And that the French were almost ten to one,
Before we met, or that a stroke was given,
Like to a trusty squire did run away :
In which assault we lost twelve hundred men ;
Myself, and divers gentlemen beside,
Were there surpris'd and taken prisoners.
Then judge, great lords, if I have done amiss ;
Or whether that such cowards ought to wear
This ornament of knighthood, yea or no.

Glo. To say the truth, this fact was infamous   30
And ill beseeming any common man ;
Much more a knight, a captain, and a leader.

Tal. When first this order was ordain'd, my lords,

Knights of the garter were of noble birth,
Valiant, and virtuous, full of haughty courage,
Such as were grown to credit by the wars ;
Not fearing death, nor shrinking for distress,
But always resolute in most extremes.
He then, that is not furnish'd in this sort,
Doth but usurp the sacred name of knight,   40
Profaning this most honourable order,
And should, if I were worthy to be judge,
Be quite degraded, like a hedge-born swain,
That doth presume to boast of gentle blood.

King. Stain to thy countrymen, thou hear'st thy doom !
Be packing therefore, thou that wast a knight :
Henceforth we banish thee on pain of death.

                              Exit Fastolfe

And now, my lord protector, view the letter
Sent from our uncle Duke of Burgundy.

Glo. What means his grace that he hath chang'd his style ?   50
No more but plain and bluntly, ' To the king ! '
Hath he forgot he is his sovereign ?
Or doth this churlish superscription
Pretend some alteration in good will ?
What 's here ?   (*reads*) ' I have, upon especial cause,
Mov'd with compassion of my country's wreck,
Together with the pitiful complaints

75

Of such as your oppression feeds upon,
Forsaken your pernicious faction,
And join'd with Charles, the rightful King of France.' 60
O monstrous treachery ! can this be so,
That in alliance, amity, and oaths,
There should be found such false dissembling guile ?

King. What ? doth my uncle Burgundy revolt ?

Glo. He doth, my lord, and is become your foe.

King. Is that the worst this letter doth contain ?

Glo. It is the worst, and all, my lord, he writes.

King. Why, then, Lord Talbot there shall talk with him,
And give him chastisement for this abuse.
How say you, my lord ? are you not content ? 70

Tal. Content, my liege ? yes, but that I am prevented,
I should have begg'd I might have been employ'd.

King. Then gather strength, and march unto him straight :
Let him perceive how ill we brook his treason,
And what offence it is to flout his friends.

Tal. I go, my lord, in heart desiring still
You may behold confusion of your foes.   *Exit*

Enter Vernon and Basset

Ver. Grant me the combat, gracious sovereign.

Bas. And me, my lord, grant me the combat too.

Yo. This is my servant, hear him, noble prince. 80

Som. And this is mine, sweet Henry, favour him.

King. Be patient, lords, and give them leave to speak.
  Say, gentlemen, what makes you thus exclaim?
  And wherefore crave you combat? or with whom?

Ver. With him, my lord, for he hath done me wrong.

Bas. And I with him; for he hath done me wrong.

King. What is that wrong, whereof you both complain?
  First let me know, and then I'll answer you.

Bas. Crossing the sea from England into France,
  This fellow here, with envious carping tongue,   90
  Upbraided me about the rose I wear,
  Saying, the sanguine colour of the leaves
  Did represent my master's blushing cheeks,
  When stubbornly he did repugn the truth
  About a certain question in the law
  Argued betwixt the Duke of York and him;
  With other vile and ignominious terms:
  In confutation of which rude reproach,
  And in defence of my lord's worthiness,
  I crave the benefit of law of arms.   100

Ver. And that is my petition, noble lord:
  For though he seem with forged quaint conceit
  To set a gloss upon his bold intent,
  Yet know, my lord, I was provok'd by him,
  And he first took exceptions at this badge,
  Pronouncing that the paleness of this flower

Bewray'd the faintness of my master's heart.

Yo. Will not this malice, Somerset, be left ?

Som. Your private grudge, my Lord of York, will out,
    Though ne'er so cunningly you smother it.   110

King. Good Lord, what madness rules in brainsick men,
    When for so slight and frivolous a cause
    Such factious emulations shall arise !
    Good cousins both, of York and Somerset,
    Quiet yourselves, I pray, and be at peace.

Yo. Let this dissension first be tried by fight,
    And then your highness shall command a peace.

Som. The quarrel toucheth none but us alone,
    Betwixt ourselves let us decide it then.

Yo. There is my pledge, accept it, Somerset.   120

Ver. Nay, let it rest where it began at first.

Bas. Confirm it so, mine honourable lord.

Glo. Confirm it so ?   Confounded be your strife,
    And perish ye, with your audacious prate !
    Presumptuous vassals, are you not asham'd
    With this immodest clamorous outrage
    To trouble and disturb the king and us ?
    And you, my lords, methinks you do not well
    To bear with their perverse objections ;
    Much less to take occasion from their mouths   130
    To raise a mutiny betwixt yourselves :

Let me persuade you take a better course.

Exe. It grieves his highness : good my lords, be friends.

King. Come hither, you that would be combatants :
  Henceforth I charge you, as you love our favour,
  Quite to forget this quarrel, and the cause.
  And you, my lords, remember where we are,
  In France, amongst a fickle wavering nation :
  If they perceive dissension in our looks,
  And that within ourselves we disagree,   140
  How will their grudging stomachs be provok'd
  To wilful disobedience, and rebel !
  Beside, what infamy will there arise,
  When foreign princes shall be certified
  That for a toy, a thing of no regard,
  King Henry's peers and chief nobility
  Destroy'd themselves, and lost the realm of France !
  O, think upon the conquest of my father,
  My tender years, and let us not forgo
  That for a trifle that was bought with blood !   150
  Let me be umpire in this doubtful strife ;
  I see no reason, if I wear this rose,

                              Putting on a red rose

  That any one should therefore be suspicious
  I more incline to Somerset than York :
  Both are my kinsmen, and I love them both :

As well they may upbraid me with my crown,
Because, forsooth, the king of Scots is crown'd.
But your discretions better can persuade
Than I am able to instruct or teach :
And therefore, as we hither came in peace,   160
So let us still continue peace and love.
Cousin of York, we institute your grace
To be our regent in these parts of France :
And, good my Lord of Somerset, unite
Your troops of horsemen with his bands of foot ;
And, like true subjects, sons of your progenitors,
Go cheerfully together, and digest
Your angry choler on your enemies.
Ourself, my lord protector, and the rest
After some respite will return to Calais ;   170
From thence to England, where I hope ere long
To be presented, by your victories,
With Charles, Alençon, and that traitorous rout.

       Flourish.   Exeunt all but York, Warwick,
                                    Exeter and Vernon

*War.*My Lord of York, I promise you, the king
    Prettily, methought, did play the orator.
Yo. And so he did ; but yet I like it not,
    In that he wears the badge of Somerset.
*War.*Tush, that was but his fancy, blame him not ;

I dare presume, sweet prince, he thought no harm.

Yo. An if I wist he did,—but let it rest ;   180
Other affairs must now be managed.

Exeunt all but Exeter

Exe. Well didst thou, Richard, to suppress thy voice ;
For, had the passions of thy heart burst out,
I fear we should have seen decipher'd there
More rancorous spite, more furious raging broils,
Than yet can be imagin'd or suppos'd.
But howsoe'er, no simple man that sees
This jarring discord of nobility,
This shouldering of each other in the court,
This factious bandying of their favourites,   190
But that it doth presage some ill event.
'Tis much when sceptres are in children's hands ;
But more, when envy breeds unkind division,
There comes the ruin, there begins confusion. *Exit*

SCENE II

Before Bourdeaux

Enter Talbot, with trump and drum

Tal. Go to the gates of Bourdeaux, trumpeter,
Summon their general unto the wall.

Trumpet sounds.   Enter General and others, aloft

English John Talbot, captains, calls you forth,
Servant in arms to Harry King of England,
And thus he would : Open your city-gates,
Be humble to us, call my sovereign yours,
And do him homage as obedient subjects,
And I 'll withdraw me and my bloody power :
But, if you frown upon this proffer'd peace,
You tempt the fury of my three attendants,   10
Lean famine, quartering steel, and climbing fire,
Who in a moment, even with the earth,
Shall lay your stately and air-braving towers,
If you forsake the offer of their love.

Gen. Thou ominous and fearful owl of death,
Our nation's terror, and their bloody scourge,
The period of thy tyranny approacheth.
On us thou canst not enter but by death ;
For I protest we are well fortified
And strong enough to issue out and fight :   20
If thou retire, the Dauphin, well appointed,
Stands with the snares of war to tangle thee :
On either hand thee there are squadrons pitch'd,
To wall thee from the liberty of flight ;
And no way canst thou turn thee for redress,
But death doth front thee with apparent spoil,

82

And pale destruction meets thee in the face :
Ten thousand French have ta'en the sacrament
To rive their dangerous artillery
Upon no Christian soul but English Talbot.   30
Lo, there thou stand'st, a breathing valiant man,
Of an invincible unconquer'd spirit !
This is the latest glory of thy praise,
That I, thy enemy, due thee withal ;
For ere the glass that now begins to run
Finish the process of his sandy hour,
These eyes, that see thee now well coloured,
Shall see thee wither'd, bloody, pale, and dead.

        Drum afar off

Hark ! hark ! the Dauphin's drum, a warning bell,
Sings heavy music to thy timorous soul,   40
And mine shall ring thy dire departure out.

        Exeunt General, &c.

Tal. He fables not, I hear the enemy :
Out, some light horsemen, and peruse their wings.
O, negligent and heedless discipline !
How are we park'd and bounded in a pale,
A little herd of England's timorous deer,
Maz'd with a yelping kennel of French curs !
If we be English deer, be then in blood,
Not rascal-like, to fall down with a pinch,

But rather moody, mad and desperate stags,5
Turn on the bloody hounds with heads of steel,
And make the cowards stand aloof at bay :
Sell every man his life as dear as mine,
And they shall find dear deer of us, my friends.
God and Saint George, Talbot and England's right,
Prosper our colours in this dangerous fight ! *Exeunt*

SCENE III

Plains in Gascony

*Enter a Messenger that meets York.   Enter York with
trumpet and many Soldiers*

Yo. Are not the speedy scouts return'd again,
That dogg'd the mighty army of the Dauphin ?
Mes. They are return'd, my lord, and give it out
That he is march'd to Bourdeaux with his power,
To fight with Talbot : as he march'd along,
By your espials were discovered
Two mightier troops than that the Dauphin led,
Which join'd with him, and made their march for
Bourdeaux.
Yo. A plague upon that villain Somerset,
That thus delays my promised supply10

    Of horsemen, that were levied for this siege!
    Renowned Talbot doth expect my aid,
    And I am lowted by a traitor villain,
    And cannot help the noble chevalier:
    God comfort him in this necessity!
    If he miscarry, farewell wars in France.

        Enter Sir William Lucy

u. Thou princely leader of our English strength,
    Never so needful on the earth of France,
    Spur to the rescue of the noble Talbot,
    Who now is girdled with a waist of iron,   20
    And hemm'd about with grim destruction:
    To Bourdeaux, warlike duke! to Bourdeaux, York!
    Else, farewell Talbot, France, and England's honour.

o. O God, that Somerset, who in proud heart
    Doth stop my cornets, were in Talbot's place!
    So should we save a valiant gentleman
    By forfeiting a traitor and a coward.
    Mad ire and wrathful fury makes me weep,
    That thus we die, while remiss traitors sleep.

u. O, send some succour to the distress'd lord!   30

o. He dies, we lose; I break my warlike word;
    We mourn, France smiles; we lose, they daily get;
    All long of this vile traitor Somerset.

u. Then God take mercy on brave Talbot's soul,

And on his son young John, who two hours since
I met in travel toward his warlike father !
This seven years did not Talbot see his son,
And now they meet where both their lives are done.

Yo. Alas, what joy shall noble Talbot have
To bid his young son welcome to his grave ?   4
Away ! vexation almost stops my breath,
That sunder'd friends greet in the hour of death.
Lucy, farewell : no more my fortune can,
But curse the cause I cannot aid the man.
Maine, Blois, Poictiers, and Tours, are won away,
Long all of Somerset and his delay.

Exit, with his soldiers

Lu. Thus, while the vulture of sedition
Feeds in the bosom of such great commanders,
Sleeping neglection doth betray to loss
The conquest of our scarce cold conqueror,   5
That ever living man of memory,
Henry the Fifth : whiles they each other cross,
Lives, honours, lands, and all, hurry to loss.   *Exit*

SCENE IV

Other plains in Gascony

*Enter Somerset, with his army ; a Captain of Talbot's
with him*

om. It is too late, I cannot send them now :
This expedition was by York and Talbot
Too rashly plotted : all our general force
Might with a sally of the very town
Be buckled with : the over-daring Talbot
Hath sullied all his gloss of former honour
By this unheedful, desperate, wild adventure :
York set him on to fight, and die in shame,
That, Talbot dead, great York might bear the name.

Cap. Here is Sir William Lucy, who with me   10
Set from our o'er-match'd forces forth for aid.

Enter Sir William Lucy

om. How now, Sir William, whither were you sent ?

Lu. Whither, my lord ? from bought and sold Lord Talbot,
Who, ring'd about with bold adversity,
Cries out for noble York and Somerset,
To beat assailing death from his weak legions :   †
And whiles the honourable captain there
Drops bloody sweat from his war-wearied limbs,

And, in advantage lingering, looks for rescue,
You, his false hopes, the trust of England's honour,
Keep off aloof with worthless emulation.
Let not your private discord keep away
The levied succours that should lend him aid,
While he, renowned noble gentleman,
Yields up his life unto a world of odds :
Orleans the Bastard, Charles, Burgundy,
Alençon, Reignier, compass him about,
And Talbot perisheth by your default.

Som. York set him on, York should have sent him aid.

Lu. And York as fast upon your grace exclaims,
Swearing that you withhold his levied host,
Collected for this expedition.

Som. York lies ; he might have sent and had the horse :
I owe him little duty, and less love,
And take foul scorn to fawn on him by sending.

Lu. The fraud of England, not the force of France,
Hath now entrapp'd the noble-minded Talbot :
Never to England shall he bear his life ;
But dies, betray'd to fortune by your strife.

Som. Come, go, I will dispatch the horsemen straight :
Within six hours they will be at his aid.

Lu. Too late comes rescue ; he is ta'en or slain,
For fly he could not, if he would have fled ;

And fly would Talbot never, though he might.

om. If he be dead, brave Talbot then adieu !

u. His fame lives in the world ; his shame in you.

Exeunt

SCENE V

The English camp near Bourdeaux

Enter Talbot and John his son

al. O young John Talbot, I did send for thee
　　To tutor thee in stratagems of war,
　　That Talbot's name might be in thee reviv'd,
　　When sapless age and weak unable limbs
　　Should bring thy father to his drooping chair.
　　But, O malignant and ill-boding stars !
　　Now thou art come unto a feast of death,
　　A terrible and unavoided danger :
　　Therefore, dear boy, mount on my swiftest horse,
　　And I 'll direct thee how thou shalt escape　　10
　　By sudden flight : come, dally not, be gone.

J.T. Is my name Talbot ? and am I your son ?
　　And shall I fly ? O, if you love my mother,
　　Dishonour not her honourable name,
　　To make a bastard and a slave of me !
　　The world will say, he is not Talbot's blood,

89

That basely fled when noble Talbot stood.

Tal. Fly, to revenge my death, if I be slain.

J.T. He that flies so will ne'er return again.

Tal. If we both stay, we both are sure to die.

J.T. Then let me stay, and, father, do you fly:
Your loss is great, so your regard should be;
My worth unknown, no loss is known in me.
Upon my death the French can little boast;
In yours they will, in you all hopes are lost.
Flight cannot stain the honour you have won,
But mine it will, that no exploit have done:
You fled for vantage, every one will swear;
But, if I bow, they 'll say it was for fear.
There is no hope that ever I will stay,
If the first hour I shrink and run away.
Here on my knee I beg mortality,
Rather than life preserv'd with infamy.

Tal. Shall all thy mother's hopes lie in one tomb?

J.T. Ay, rather than I 'll shame my mother's womb.

Tal. Upon my blessing, I command thee go.

J.T. To fight I will, but not to fly the foe.

Tal. Part of thy father may be sav'd in thee.

J.T. No part of him but will be shame in me.

Tal. Thou never hadst renown, nor canst not lose it.

J.T. Yes, your renowned name: shall flight abuse it?

Tal. Thy father's charge shall clear thee from that stain.

J.T. You cannot witness for me, being slain.
If death be so apparent, then both fly.

Tal. And leave my followers here to fight and die?
My age was never tainted with such shame.

J.T. And shall my youth be guilty of such blame?
No more can I be sever'd from your side,
Than can yourself yourself in twain divide:
Stay, go, do what you will, the like do I;   50
For live I will not, if my father die.

Tal. Then here I take my leave of thee, fair son,   †
Born to eclipse thy life this afternoon.
Come, side by side, together live and die,
And soul with soul from France to heaven fly.

Exeunt

SCENE VI

A field of battle

*Alarum : excursions, wherein Talbot's Son is hemmed
about, and Talbot rescues him*

Tal. Saint George and victory! fight, soldiers, fight:
The regent hath with Talbot broke his word,
And left us to the rage of France his sword.
Where is John Talbot?   Pause, and take thy breath;

       I gave thee life and rescued thee from death.

J.T. O, twice my father, twice am I thy son !
       The life thou gav'st me first was lost and done,
       Till with thy warlike sword, despite of fate,
       To my determin'd time thou gav'st new date.

Tal. When from the Dauphin's crest thy sword struck fire, 10
       It warm'd thy father's heart with proud desire
       Of bold-fac'd victory.   Then leaden age,
       Quicken'd with youthful spleen and warlike rage,
       Beat down Alençon, Orleans, Burgundy,
       And from the pride of Gallia rescued thee.
       The ireful bastard Orleans, that drew blood
       From thee, my boy, and had the maidenhood
       Of thy first fight, I soon encountered,
       And interchanging blows I quickly shed
       Some of his bastard blood, and in disgrace   20
       Bespoke him thus ; ' Contaminated, base,
       And misbegotten blood I spill of thine,
       Mean and right poor, for that pure blood of mine,
       Which thou didst force from Talbot, my brave boy : '
       Here, purposing the Bastard to destroy,
       Came in strong rescue.   Speak, thy father's care,
       Art thou not weary, John ? how dost thou fare ?
       Wilt thou yet leave the battle, boy, and fly,
       Now thou art seal'd the son of chivalry ?

Fly, to revenge my death when I am dead :   30
The help of one stands me in little stead.
O, too much folly is it, well I wot,
To hazard all our lives in one small boat !
If I to-day die not with Frenchmen's rage,
To-morrow I shall die with mickle age :
By me they nothing gain, an if I stay,
'Tis but the shortening of my life one day :
In thee thy mother dies, our household's name,
My death's revenge, thy youth, and England's fame :
All these, and more, we hazard by thy stay ;   40
All these are sav'd if thou wilt fly away.

J.T.   The sword of Orleans hath not made me smart ;
These words of yours draw life-blood from my heart :
On that advantage, bought with such a shame,
To save a paltry life, and slay bright fame,
Before young Talbot from old Talbot fly,
The coward horse that bears me fall and die !
And like me to the peasant boys of France,
To be shame's scorn, and subject of mischance !
Surely, by all the glory you have won,   50
An if I fly, I am not Talbot's son :
Then talk no more of flight, it is no boot ;
If son to Talbot, die at Talbot's foot.

Tal.   Then follow thou thy desperate sire of Crete,

Thou Icarus ; thy life to me is sweet :
If thou wilt fight, fight by thy father's side,
And commendable prov'd, let 's die in pride.

Exeunt

SCENE VII

Another part of the field

Alarum : excursions.   Enter old Talbot led by a Servant

Tal. Where is my other life ? mine own is gone ;
O, where 's young Talbot ? where is valiant John ?
Triumphant death, smear'd with captivity,
Young Talbot's valour makes me smile at thee :
When he perceiv'd me shrink, and on my knee,
His bloody sword he brandish'd over me,
And, like a hungry lion, did commence
Rough deeds of rage and stern impatience ;
But when my angry guardant stood alone,
Tendering my ruin, and assail'd of none,   10
Dizzy-eyed fury and great rage of heart
Suddenly made him from my side to start
Into the clustering battle of the French ;
And in that sea of blood my boy did drench
His over-mounting spirit ; and there died,
My Icarus, my blossom, in his pride.

Ser. O my dear lord, lo, where your son is borne !
　　　Enter Soldiers, with the body of young Talbot

Tal. Thou antic death, which laugh'st us here to scorn,
　　　Anon, from thy insulting tyranny,
　　　Coupled in bonds of perpetuity,　　　　　　　　　20
　　　Two Talbots, winged through the lither sky,
　　　In thy despite shall 'scape mortality.
　　　O thou, whose wounds become hard-favour'd death,
　　　Speak to thy father ere thou yield thy breath !
　　　Brave death by speaking, whether he will or no ;
　　　Imagine him a Frenchman, and thy foe.
　　　Poor boy ! he smiles, methinks, as who should say,
　　　' Had death been French, then death had died to-day.'
　　　Come, come and lay him in his father's arms :
　　　My spirit can no longer bear these harms.　　　30
　　　Soldiers, adieu !   I have what I would have,
　　　Now my old arms are young John Talbot's grave.
　　　　　　　　　　　　　　　　　　　　　Dies

　　　Enter Charles, Alençon, Burgundy, Bastard,
　　　　　　La Pucelle, and forces

Cha. Had York and Somerset brought rescue in,
　　　We should have found a bloody day of this.

Orl. How the young whelp of Talbot's, raging wood,
　　　Did flesh his puny sword in Frenchmen's blood !

Joan. Once I encounter'd him, and thus I said :

'Thou maiden youth, be vanquish'd by a maid:'
But, with a proud majestical high scorn,
He answer'd thus: 'Young Talbot was not born   40
To be the pillage of a giglot wench:'
So, rushing in the bowels of the French,
He left me proudly, as unworthy fight.

Bur. Doubtless he would have made a noble knight:
See, where he lies inhearsed in the arms
Of the most bloody nurser of his harms!

Orl. Hew them to pieces, hack their bones asunder,
Whose life was England's glory, Gallia's wonder.

Cha. O, no, forbear! for that which we have fled
During the life, let us not wrong it dead.   50

*Enter Sir William Lucy, attended; Herald of the
French preceding*

Lu. Herald, conduct me to the Dauphin's tent,
To know who hath obtain'd the glory of the day.

Cha. On what submissive message art thou sent?

Lu. Submission, Dauphin! 'tis a mere French word;
We English warriors wot not what it means.
I come to know what prisoners thou hast ta'en,
And to survey the bodies of the dead.

Cha. For prisoners ask'st thou? hell our prison is.
But tell me whom thou seek'st.

Lu. But where's the great Alcides of the field,   †

Valiant Lord Talbot, Earl of Shrewsbury,   61
Created, for his rare success in arms,
Great Earl of Washford, Waterford and Valence,
Lord Talbot of Goodrig and Urchinfield,
Lord Strange of Blackmere, Lord Verdun of Alton,
Lord Cromwell of Wingfield, Lord Furnival of
      Sheffield,
The thrice-victorious Lord of Falconbridge ;
Knight of the noble order of Saint George,
Worthy Saint Michael and the Golden Fleece ;
Great marshal to Henry the Sixth   70
Of all his wars within the realm of France ?

Joan. Here is a silly stately style indeed !
The Turk, that two and fifty kingdoms hath,
Writes not so tedious a style as this.
Him that thou magnifiest with all these titles
Stinking and fly-blown lies here at our feet.

Lu. Is Talbot slain, the Frenchmen's only scourge,
Your kingdom's terror, and black Nemesis ?
O, were mine eye-balls into bullets turn'd,
That I in rage might shoot them at your faces !   80
O, that I could but call these dead to life !
It were enough to fright the realm of France :
Were but his picture left amongst you here,
It would amaze the proudest of you all.

Give me their bodies, that I may bear them hence,
And give them burial as beseems their worth.

Joan. I think this upstart is old Talbot's ghost,
He speaks with such a proud commanding spirit.
For God's sake, let him have 'em ; to keep them here,
They would but stink, and putrefy the air.　　　　90

Cha. Go, take their bodies hence.

Lu. I'll bear them hence ; but from their ashes shall be
　　　rear'd
A phœnix that shall make all France afeard.

Cha. So we be rid of them, do with 'em what thou wilt.
And now to Paris, in this conquering vein :
All will be ours, now bloody Talbot's slain. *Exeunt*

Act Fifth

SCENE I

London.　The palace

Sennet.　Enter King, Gloucester, and Exeter

King. Have you perus'd the letters from the pope,
The emperor, and the Earl of Armagnac ?

Glo. I have, my lord, and their intent is this :

They humbly sue unto your excellence
To have a godly peace concluded of,
Between the realms of England and of France.

King. How doth your grace affect their motion ?

Glo. Well, my good lord, and as the only means
To stop effusion of our Christian blood,
And stablish quietness on every side.   10

King. Ay, marry, uncle, for I always thought
It was both impious and unnatural
That such immanity and bloody strife
Should reign among professors of one faith.

Glo. Beside, my lord, the sooner to effect
And surer bind this knot of amity,
The Earl of Armagnac, near knit to Charles,
A man of great authority in France,
Proffers his only daughter to your grace
In marriage, with a large and sumptuous dowry.   20

King. Marriage, uncle ! alas, my years are young !
And fitter is my study, and my books,
Than wanton dalliance with a paramour.
Yet call the ambassadors, and, as you please,
So let them have their answers every one :
I shall be well content with any choice
Tends to God's glory and my country's weal.

99

*Enter Winchester in Cardinal's habit, a Legate
and two Ambassadors*

Exe. What ? is my Lord of Winchester install'd,
    And call'd unto a cardinal's degree ?
    Then I perceive that will be verified   30
    Henry the Fifth did sometime prophesy,
    ' If once he come to be a cardinal,
    He'll make his cap co-equal with the crown.'

King. My lords ambassadors, your several suits
    Have been consider'd and debated on ;
    Your purpose is both good and reasonable ;
    And therefore are we certainly resolv'd
    To draw conditions of a friendly peace,
    Which by my Lord of Winchester we mean
    Shall be transported presently to France.   40

Glo. And for the proffer of my lord your master,
    I have inform'd his highness so at large,
    As liking of the lady's virtuous gifts,
    Her beauty, and the value of her dower,
    He doth intend she shall be England's queen.

King. In argument and proof of which contract,
    Bear her this jewel, pledge of my affection,
    And so, my lord protector, see them guarded,
    And safely brought to Dover, wherein shipp'd

Commit them to the fortune of the sea.   50
     Exeunt all but Winchester and Legate

Win. Stay, my lord legate, you shall first receive
 The sum of money which I promised
 Should be deliver'd to his holiness
 For clothing me in these grave ornaments.

Leg. I will attend upon your lordship's leisure.

Win. *(aside)* Now Winchester will not submit, I trow,
 Or be inferior to the proudest peer.
 Humphrey of Gloucester, thou shalt well perceive
 That neither in birth, or for authority,
 The bishop will be overborne by thee :   60
 I'll either make thee stoop, and bend thy knee,
 Or sack this country with a mutiny. *Exeunt*

SCENE II

France. Plains in Anjou

Enter Charles, Burgundy, Alençon, Bastard, Reignier,
La Pucelle, and forces

Cha. These news, my lords, may cheer our drooping
  spirits :
 'Tis said the stout Parisians do revolt
 And turn again unto the warlike French.

Al. Then march to Paris, royal Charles of France,
 And keep not back your powers in dalliance.

Joan. Peace be amongst them, if they turn to us,
 Else, ruin combat with their palaces !

     Enter Scout

Scout. Success unto our valiant general,
 And happiness to his accomplices !

Cha. What tidings send our scouts ? I prithee speak. 10

Scout. The English army, that divided was
 Into two parties, is now conjoin'd in one,
 And means to give you battle presently.

Cha. Somewhat too sudden, sirs, the warning is,
 But we will presently provide for them.

Bur. I trust the ghost of Talbot is not there :
 Now he is gone, my lord, you need not fear.

Joan. Of all base passions, fear is most accurs'd.
 Command the conquest, Charles, it shall be thine,
 Let Henry fret and all the world repine. 20

Cha. Then on, my lords, and France be fortunate !

       Exeunt

SCENE III

Before Angiers

Alarum.   Excursions.   Enter La Pucelle

Joan. The regent conquers, and the Frenchmen fly.
   Now help, ye charming spells and periapts,
   And ye choice spirits that admonish me,
   And give me signs of future accidents.   *Thunder*
   You speedy helpers, that are substitutes
   Under the lordly monarch of the north,
   Appear, and aid me in this enterprise.
               Enter Fiends
   This speedy and quick appearance argues proof
   Of your accustom'd diligence to me.
   Now, ye familiar spirits, that are cull'd   10
   Out of the powerful regions under earth,
   Help me this once, that France may get the field.
                  They walk, and speak not
   O, hold me not with silence over-long !
   Where I was wont to feed you with my blood,
   I'll lop a member off, and give it you,
   In earnest of a further benefit,
   So you do condescend to help me now.
                  They hang their heads

No hope to have redress ?　My body shall
Pay recompense, if you will grant my suit.

They shake their heads

Cannot my body, nor blood-sacrifice,
Entreat you to your wonted furtherance ?
Then take my soul, my body, soul and all,
Before that England give the French the foil.

They depart

See, they forsake me !　Now the time is come
That France must vail her lofty-plumed crest,
And let her head fall into England's lap.
My ancient incantations are too weak,
And hell too strong for me to buckle with :
Now, France, thy glory droopeth to the dust. *Exit*

*Excursions.　Re-enter La Pucelle fighting hand to hand
with York : La Pucelle is taken.　The French fly*

Yo. Damsel of France, I think I have you fast :
Unchain your spirits now with spelling charms,
And try if they can gain your liberty.
A goodly prize, fit for the devil's grace !
See, how the ugly witch doth bend her brows,
As if with Circe she would change my shape !

Joan. Chang'd to a worser shape thou canst not be.

Yo. O, Charles the Dauphin is a proper man ;
No shape but his can please your dainty eye.

an. A plaguing mischief light on Charles and thee !
　　And may ye both be suddenly surpris'd　　　　40
　　By bloody hands, in sleeping on your beds !

o. Fell banning hag, enchantress, hold thy tongue !

an. I prithee, give me leave to curse awhile.

o. Curse, miscreant, when thou comest to the stake.

　　　　　　　　　　　　　　　　Exeunt

　　Alarum.   Enter Suffolk, with Margaret in his hand

uf. Be what thou wilt, thou art my prisoner.

　　　　　　　　　　　　　　Gazes on her

　　O fairest beauty, do not fear, nor fly !
　　For I will touch thee but with reverent hands ;
　　I kiss these fingers for eternal peace,
　　And lay them gently on thy tender side.
　　Who art thou ? say, that I may honour thee.　　50

Mar. Margaret my name, and daughter to a king,
　　The King of Naples, whosoe'er thou art.

uf. An earl I am, and Suffolk am I call'd.
　　Be not offended, nature's miracle,
　　Thou art allotted to be ta'en by me :
　　So doth the swan her downy cygnets save,
　　Keeping them prisoner underneath her wings.
　　Yet, if this servile usage once offend,
　　Go and be free again as Suffolk's friend. *She is going*
　　O, stay !   I have no power to let her pass,　　60

105

My hand would free her, but my heart says no.
As plays the sun upon the glassy streams,
Twinkling another counterfeited beam,
So seems this gorgeous beauty to mine eyes.
Fain would I woo her, yet I dare not speak :
I'll call for pen and ink, and write my mind.
Fie, de la Pole ! disable not thyself ;
Hast not a tongue ? is she not here ?
Wilt thou be daunted at a woman's sight ?
Ay, beauty's princely majesty is such,   7⁰
Confounds the tongue and make the senses rough.

Mar. Say, Earl of Suffolk,—if thy name be so—
What ransom must I pay before I pass ?
For I perceive I am thy prisoner.

Suf. How canst thou tell she will deny thy suit,
Before thou make a trial of her love ?

Mar. Why speak'st thou not ? what ransom must I pay ?

Suf. She's beautiful ; and therefore to be woo'd :
She is a woman ; therefore to be won.

Mar. Wilt thou accept of ransom, yea nor no ?   8⁰

Suf. Fond man, remember that thou hast a wife,
Then how can Margaret be thy paramour ?

Mar. I were best to leave him, for he will not hear.

Suf. There all is marr'd ; there lies a cooling card.

Mar. He talks at random ; sure, the man is mad.

Suf. And yet a dispensation **may be had.**

Mar. And yet I would that you would answer me.

Suf. I'll win this Lady Margaret.   For whom?
  Why, for my king: tush, that's a wooden thing!

Mar. He talks of wood: it is some carpenter.   90

Suf. Yet so my fancy may be satisfied,
  And peace established between these realms.
  But there remains a scruple in that too;
  For though her father be the King of Naples,
  Duke of Anjou and Maine, yet is he poor,
  And our nobility will scorn the match.

Mar. Hear ye, captain, are you not at leisure?

Suf. It shall be so, disdain they ne'er so much:
  Henry is youthful, and will quickly yield.
  Madam, I have a secret to reveal.   100

Mar. What though I be enthrall'd? he seems a knight,
  And will not any way dishonour me.

Suf. Lady, vouchsafe to listen what I say.

Mar. Perhaps I shall be rescued by the French;
  And then I need not crave his courtesy.

Suf. Sweet madam, give me hearing in a cause—

Mar. Tush, women have been captivate ere now.

Suf. Lady, wherefore talk you so?

Mar. I cry you mercy, 'tis but Quid for Quo.

Suf. Say, gentle princess, would you not suppose   110

Your bondage happy, to be made a queen?

Mar. To be a queen in bondage is more vile
Than is a slave in base servility;
For princes should be free.

Suf.   And so shall you,
If happy England's royal king be free.

Mar. Why, what concerns his freedom unto me?

Suf. I'll undertake to make thee Henry's queen,
To put a golden sceptre in thy hand,
And set a precious crown upon thy head,
If thou wilt condescend to be my—

Mar.   What?   12

Suf. His love.

Mar. I am unworthy to be Henry's wife.

Suf. No, gentle madam, I unworthy am
To woo so fair a dame to be his wife,
And have no portion in the choice myself.
How say you, madam, are ye so content?

Mar. An if my father please, I am content.

Suf. Then call our captains and our colours forth,
And, madam, at your father's castle walls
We'll crave a parley, to confer with him.   13

> *A parley sounded.   Enter Reignier on the walls*

See, Reignier, see, thy daughter prisoner!

Rei. To whom?

Suf.   To me.

Rei.   Suffolk, what remedy?
I am a soldier, and unapt to weep,
Or to exclaim on fortune's fickleness.

Suf. Yes, there is remedy enough, my lord:
Consent, and for thy honour give consent,
Thy daughter shall be wedded to my king,
Whom I with pain have woo'd and won thereto;
And this her easy-held imprisonment
Hath gain'd thy daughter princely liberty.   140

Rei. Speaks Suffolk as he thinks?

Suf.   Fair Margaret knows
That Suffolk doth not flatter, face, or feign.

Rei. Upon thy princely warrant, I descend
To give thee answer of thy just demand.

Exit from the walls

Suf. And here I will expect thy coming.

Trumpets sound.   Enter Reignier, below

Rei. Welcome, brave earl, into our territories:
Command in Anjou what your honour pleases.

Suf. Thanks, Reignier, happy for so sweet a child,
Fit to be made companion with a king:
What answer makes your grace unto my suit?   150

Rei. Since thou dost deign to woo her little worth
To be the princely bride of such a lord;

       Upon condition I may quietly
       Enjoy mine own, the country Maine and Anjou,
       Free from oppression or the stroke of war,
       My daughter shall be Henry's, if he please.

Suf. That is her ransom ; I deliver her ;
       And those two counties I will undertake
       Your grace shall well and quietly enjoy.

Rei. And I again, in Henry's royal name,   160
       As deputy unto that gracious king,
       Give thee her hand, for sign of plighted faith.

Suf. Reignier of France, I give thee kingly thanks,
       Because this is in traffic of a king.
       (*aside*) And yet, methinks, I could be well content
       To be mine own attorney in this case.
       I'll over then to England with this news,
       And make this marriage to be solemnized.
       So farewell, Reignier, set this diamond safe
       In golden palaces, as it becomes.   170

Rei. I do embrace thee, as I would embrace
       The Christian prince, King Henry, were he here.

Mar. Farewell, my lord : good wishes, praise and prayers,
       Shall Suffolk ever have of Margaret.   *Going*

Suf. Farewell, sweet madam : but hark you, Margaret,
       No princely commendations to my king ?

Mar. Such commendations as becomes a maid,

    A virgin, and his servant, say to him.

Suf. Words sweetly plac'd and modestly directed.

    But, madam, I must trouble you again,   180

    No loving token to his majesty?

Mar. Yes, my good lord, a pure unspotted heart,

    Never yet taint with love, I send the king.

Suf. And this withal.   *Kisses her*

Mar. That for thyself!   I will not so presume

    To send such peevish tokens to a king.

               Exeunt Reignier and Margaret

Suf. O, wert thou for myself!   But, Suffolk, stay;

    Thou mayst not wander in that labyrinth;

    There Minotaurs and ugly treasons lurk.

    Solicit Henry with her wondrous praise: 190

    Bethink thee on her virtues that surmount,

    And natural graces that extinguish art;

    Repeat their semblance often on the seas,

    That when thou com'st to kneel at Henry's feet,

    Thou mayst bereave him of his wits with wonder.

                         Exit

SCENE IV

Camp of the Duke of York in Anjou

Enter York, Warwick, and others

Yo. Bring forth that sorceress condemn'd to burn.

        Enter La Pucelle, guarded, and a Shepherd

Shep. Ah, Joan, this kills thy father's heart outright!
Have I sought every country far and near,
And now it is my chance to find thee out,
Must I behold thy timeless cruel death?
Ah, Joan, sweet daughter Joan, I'll die with thee!

Joan. Decrepit miser! base ignoble wretch!
I am descended of a gentler blood:
Thou art no father nor no friend of mine.

Shep. Out, out! My lords, an please you, 'tis not so;   10
I did beget her, all the parish knows:
Her mother liveth yet, can testify
She was the first fruit of my bachelorship.

War. Graceless! wilt thou deny thy parentage?

Yo. This argues what her kind of life hath been,
Wicked and vile, and so her death concludes.

Shep. Fie, Joan, that thou wilt be so obstacle!
God knows thou art a collop of my flesh,
And for thy sake have I shed many a tear:

  Deny me not, I prithee, gentle Joan.   **20**

Joan. Peasant, avaunt ! You have suborn'd this man

  Of purpose, to obscure my noble birth.

Shep. 'Tis true, I gave a noble to the priest

  The morn that I was wedded to her mother.

  Kneel down and take my blessing, good my girl.

  Wilt thou not stoop ? Now cursed be the time

  Of thy nativity ! I would the milk

  Thy mother gave thee when thou suck'st her breast,

  Had been a little ratsbane for thy sake !

  Or else, when thou didst keep my lambs a-field, **30**

  I wish some ravenous wolf had eaten thee !

  Dost thou deny thy father, cursed drab ?

  O, burn her, burn her ! hanging is too good. *Exit*

Yo. Take her away, for she hath liv'd too long,

  To fill the world with vicious qualities.

Joan. First let me tell you whom you have condemn'd :

  Not me, begotten of a shepherd swain,

  But issued from the progeny of kings ;

  Virtuous and holy, chosen from above,

  By inspiration of celestial grace,   **40**

  To work exceeding miracles on earth.

  I never had to do with wicked spirits :

  But you, that are polluted with your lusts,

  Stain'd with the guiltless blood of innocents,

Corrupt and tainted with a thousand vices,
Because you want the grace that others have,
You judge it straight a thing impossible
To compass wonders but by help of devils.
No, misconceiv'd! Joan of Arc hath been
A virgin from her tender infancy, 50
Chaste, and immaculate in very thought,
Whose maiden blood, thus rigorously effus'd,
Will cry for vengeance at the gates of heaven.

Yo. Ay, ay: away with her to execution!

War. And hark ye, sirs; because she is a maid,
Spare for no faggots, let there be enow:
Place barrels of pitch upon the fatal stake,
That so her torture may be shortened.

Joan. Will nothing turn your unrelenting hearts?
Then, Joan, discover thine infirmity, 60
That warranteth by law to be thy privilege.
I am with child, ye bloody homicides:
Murder not then the fruit within my womb,
Although ye hale me to a violent death.

Yo. Now heaven forfend! the holy maid with child?

War. The greatest miracle that e'er ye wrought:
Is all your strict preciseness come to this?

Yo. She and the Dauphin have been juggling:
I did imagine what would be her refuge.

*War.*Well, go to ; we'll have no bastards live,   70
  Especially since Charles must father it.

*Joan.*You are deceiv'd ; my child is none of his :
  It was Alençon that enjoy'd my love.

Yo. Alençon ! that notorious Machiavel !
  It dies, an if it had a thousand lives.

*Joan.*O, give me leave, I have deluded you ;
  'Twas neither Charles, nor yet the duke I nam'd,
  But Reignier, king of Naples, that prevail'd.

*War.*A married man ! that's most intolerable.

Yo. Why, here's a girl !   I think she knows not well   80
  (There were so many) whom she may accuse.

*War.*It's sign she hath been liberal and free.

Yo. And yet, forsooth, she is a virgin pure.
  Strumpet, thy words condemn thy brat, and thee :
  Use no entreaty, for it is in vain.

*Joan.*Then lead me hence ; with whom I leave my curse :
  May never glorious sun reflex his beams
  Upon the country where you make abode ;
  But darkness, and the gloomy shade of death,
  Environ you, till mischief and despair   90
  Drive you to break your necks, or hang yourselves !
        Exit, guarded

Yo. Break thou in pieces and consume to ashes,
  Thou foul accursed minister of hell !

Enter Cardinal Beaufort, Bishop of Winchester, attended

Car. Lord regent, I do greet your excellence
    With letters of commission from the king.
    For know, my lord, the states of Christendom,
    Mov'd with remorse of these outrageous broils,
    Have earnestly implor'd a general peace
    Betwixt our nation and the aspiring French ;
    And here at hand the Dauphin and his train   100
    Approacheth, to confer about some matter.

Yo. Is all our travail turn'd to this effect ?
    After the slaughter of so many peers,
    So many captains, gentlemen, and soldiers,
    That in this quarrel have been overthrown,
    And sold their bodies for their country's benefit,
    Shall we at last conclude effeminate peace ?
    Have we not lost most part of all the towns,
    By treason, falsehood, and by treachery,
    Our great progenitors had conquered ?   110
    O, Warwick, Warwick, I foresee with grief
    The utter loss of all the realm of France.

War. Be patient, York ; if we conclude a peace,
    It shall be with such strict and severe covenants
    As little shall the Frenchmen gain thereby.

Enter Charles, Alençon, Bastard, Reignier, and others

Cha. Since, lords of England, it is thus agreed,

That peaceful truce shall be proclaim'd in France,
We come to be informed by yourselves
What the conditions of that league must be.

Yo. Speak Winchester, for boiling choler chokes   120
The hollow passage of my poison'd voice,   †
By sight of these our baleful enemies.

Car. Charles, and the rest, it is enacted thus :
That, in regard King Henry gives consent,
Of mere compassion, and of lenity,
To ease your country of distressful war,
And suffer you to breathe in fruitful peace,
You shall become true liegemen to his crown :
And, Charles, upon condition thou wilt swear
To pay him tribute, and submit thyself,   130
Thou shalt be plac'd as viceroy under him,
And still enjoy thy regal dignity.

Al. Must he be then as shadow of himself ?
Adorn his temples with a coronet,
And yet, in substance and authority,
Retain but privilege of a private man ?
This proffer is absurd and reasonless.

Cha. 'Tis known already that I am possess'd
With more than half the Gallian territories,
And therein reverenc'd for their lawful king :   140
Shall I, for lucre of the rest unvanquish'd,

Detract so much from that prerogative,
As to be call'd but viceroy of the whole?
No, lord ambassador, I'll rather keep
That which I have than, coveting for more,
Be cast from possibility of all.

Yo. Insulting Charles, hast thou by secret means
Us'd intercession to obtain a league,
And, now the matter grows to compromise,
Stand'st thou aloof upon comparison?   150
Either accept the title thou usurp'st,
Of benefit proceeding from our king,
And not of any challenge of desert,
Or we will plague thee with incessant wars.

Rei. My lord, you do not well in obstinacy
To cavil in the course of this contract:
If once it be neglected, ten to one
We shall not find like opportunity.

Al. To say the truth, it is your policy
To save your subjects from such massacre   160
And ruthless slaughters as are daily seen,
By our proceeding in hostility;
And therefore take this compact of a truce,
Although you break it when your pleasure serves.

War. How say'st thou, Charles? shall our condition stand?
Cha. It shall;

Only reserv'd, you claim no interest
In any of our towns of garrison.

Yo. Then swear allegiance to his majesty,
As thou art knight, never to disobey   170
Nor be rebellious to the crown of England,
Thou, nor thy nobles, to the crown of England.
So, now dismiss your army when ye please ;
Hang up your ensigns, let your drums be still,
Fot here we entertain a solemn peace.   *Exeunt*

SCENE V

London.   The royal palace

*Enter Suffolk in conference with the King, Gloucester
and Exeter*

King. Your wondrous rare description, noble earl,
Of beauteous Margaret hath astonish'd me :
Her virtues graced with external gifts
Do breed love's settled passions in my heart,
And like as rigour of tempestuous gusts
Provokes the mightiest hulk against the tide,
So am I driven by breath of her renown,
Either to suffer shipwreck, or arrive
Where I may have fruition of her love.

Suf. Tush, my good lord, this superficial tale   10

Is but a preface of her worthy praise ;
The chief perfections of that lovely dame
(Had I sufficient skill to utter them)
Would make a volume of enticing lines,
Able to ravish any dull conceit :
And, which is more, she is not so divine,
So full-replete with choice of all delights,
But with as humble lowliness of mind
She is content to be at your command ;
Command, I mean, of virtuous chaste intents,   20
To love and honour Henry as her lord.

King. And otherwise will Henry ne'er presume.
Therefore, my lord protector, give consent
That Margaret may be England's royal queen.

Glo. So should I give consent to flatter sin.
You know, my lord, your highness is betroth'd
Unto another lady of esteem :
How shall we then dispense with that contract,
And not deface your honour with reproach ?

Suf. As doth a ruler with unlawful oaths,   30
Or one that, at a triumph having vow'd
To try his strength, forsaketh yet the lists
By reason of his adversary's odds :
A poor earl's daughter is unequal odds,
And therefore may be broke without offence.

Glo. Why, what, I pray, is Margaret more than that?
  Her father is no better than an earl,
  Although in glorious titles he excel.

Suf. Yes, my lord, her father is a king,
  The King of Naples and Jerusalem;   40
  And of such great authority in France,
  As his alliance will confirm our peace,
  And keep the Frenchman in allegiance.

Glo. And so the Earl of Armagnac may do,
  Because he is near kinsman unto Charles.

Exe. Beside, his wealth doth warrant a liberal dower,
  Where Reignier sooner will receive than give.

Suf. A dower, my lords? disgrace not so your king,
  That he should be so abject, base, and poor,
  To choose for wealth, and not for perfect love. 50
  Henry is able to enrich his queen,
  And not to seek a queen to make him rich:
  So worthless peasants bargain for their wives,
  As market-men for oxen, sheep, or horse.
  Marriage is a matter of more worth
  Than to be dealt in by attorneyship;
  Not whom we will, but whom his grace affects,
  Must be companion of his nuptial bed:
  And therefore, lords, since he affects her most,
  It most of all these reasons bindeth us, 60

In our opinions she should be preferr'd.
For what is wedlock forced but a hell,
An age of discord and continual strife?
Whereas the contrary bringeth bliss,
And is a pattern of celestial peace.
Whom should we match with Henry, being a king,
But Margaret, that is daughter to a king?
Her peerless feature, joined with her birth,
Approves her fit for none but for a king:
Her valiant courage, and undaunted spirit,
(More than in women commonly is seen)
Will answer our hope in issue of a king;
For Henry, son unto a conqueror,
Is likely to beget more conquerors,
If with a lady of so high resolve
As is fair Margaret he be link'd in love.
Then yield, my lords, and here conclude with me
That Margaret shall be queen, and none but she.

King. Whether it be through force of your report,
My noble Lord of Suffolk, or for that
My tender youth was never yet attaint
With any passion of inflaming love,
I cannot tell; but this I am assur'd,
I feel such sharp dissension in my breast,
Such fierce alarums both of hope and fear,

70

80

As I am sick with working of my thoughts.
Take, therefore, shipping, post, my lord, to France,
Agree to any covenants, and procure
That Lady Margaret do vouchsafe to come
To cross the seas to England, and be crown'd   90
King Henry's faithful and anointed queen:
For your expenses and sufficient charge,
Among the people gather up a tenth.
Be gone, I say, for, till you do return,
I rest perplexed with a thousand cares.
And you, good uncle, banish all offence:
If you do censure me by what you were,
Not what you are, I know it will excuse
This sudden execution of my will.
And so, conduct me where, from company,   100
I may revolve and ruminate my grief.   *Exit*

Glo. Ay, grief, I fear me, both at first and last.

> *Exeunt Gloucester and Exeter*

Suf. Thus Suffolk hath prevail'd, and thus he goes,
As did the youthful Paris once to Greece,
With hope to find the like event in love,
But prosper better than the Trojan did.
Margaret shall now be queen, and rule the king;
But I will rule both her, the king and realm.   *Exit*

Notes

I. i. 56. *Julius Cæsar or bright . . .*; 'there was a great comet which seven nights together was seen very bright after Cæsar's death' (Plutarch). There have been all manner of conjectures for filling up the line.

I. i. 132. *in the vaward, plac'd behind*; if this is right, and we ought not, with Theobald, boldly to read *rereward*, it must mean that he was in support of the vanguard (*i.e.* behind it, though in front of the main body).

I. ii. 21. *fly*; couplets closing sections are so common in this play that it is tempting to read *flee*.

I. ii. 48. *appall'd*; F *appal'd*, which might stand for either *appalled* or *appaled*, i.e. 'made pale.'

I. ii. 56. *nine sibyls of old Rome*; this appears to be a confusion for the nine books which the one sibyl brought for sale to Tarquin.

I. ii. 131. *St Martin's summer, halcyon days*; St Martin's summer was the Indian summer about the feast of St Martin, November 11. The halcyon days were a period of calm alleged to coincide with the sitting and hatching of the halcyons, and according to Pliny were the week before and the week after midwinter.

I. ii. 139-43. North's *Plutarch* records the story of Cæsar's adventure in a small rowing boat in a storm; the master of the pinnace wished to return; Cæsar said to him, 'Good fellow, be of good cheer and forwards hardily, fear not, for thou hast Cæsar and his fortune with thee.' Nashe speaks of 'the Dove wherewith the Turks hold Mahomet their Prophet to be inspired.' For Saint Philip's daughters see Acts xxi. 9.

I. iii. 39. *Damascus* was supposed to have been founded on the site where Abel was murdered.

I. iv. 33. *pill'd esteem'd*; F *pil'd-esteem'd*; *pil'd* is a common enough spelling of *pill'd*, i.e. 'stripped,' and I see no reason to adopt any of the numerous emendations; the usual one is *vile-esteem'd*.

I. iv. 107. *puzzel* means a drab, *dolphin* is the normal Elizabethan spelling of Dauphin, and *dog-fish* was used as a common term of abuse.

I. vi. 4. *Astræa*; the goddess of Justice (here apparently quadrisyllabic).

I. vi. 6. *Adonis' garden*; often alluded to at the time, often along with the garden or apples of the Hesperides. See in particular *The Faerie Queene*, III. vi.

I. vi. 22. *Rhodope*; there were at least two Rhodopes, and diverse accounts of one of them; but this is clearly the famous courtesan who, according to one account, ultimately married Psammetichus of Egypt, and built a pyramid. It is tempting to read *of* or *in* for *or*.

II. iii. 6. *Tomyris*, queen of the Massagetæ, defeated Cyrus and killed him.

II. iv. 117. *wip'd*; F reads *whipt*, but the later Ff were clearly unhappy about it and read *wip't*.

III. i. 63. *enter talk*; Hart suggests that we should join the words and read *entertalk*.

III. i. 134. I have restored the F punctuation. The usual punctuation puts a heavy stop after *to thee*; and though the run of F is awkward, it seems to me less awkward than to allow the 'proud prelate' to admit that he yields to Gloucester. In fact he yields to the King and Warwick.

III. ii. 18-19. Again the F punctuation. The first line is a condition: 'if Saint Denis will bless . . . we'll sleep secure in Rouen.'

III. ii. 95. *Pendragon*, i.e. Uther Pendragon, father of Arthur, who was brought to the ' field of Verolam, sicke, and in his Horse-litter.'

IV. iv. 16. *legions*; Rowe's emendation of F's *regions*, which is difficult but not impossible.

IV. v. 52. *son . . . eclipse*; the frequent quibble on ' son ' and ' sun.'

IV. vii. 60. *Alcides*; Hercules; but it is hard not to suspect a confusion, since Hercules was not primarily distinguished for his exploits ' in the field.' Pelides (Achilles) would be much more appropriate.

V. iv. 121. *poison'd*; so F. Theobald suggested *prison'd*.

Glossary

Many words and phrases in Shakespeare require glossing, not because they are in themselves unfamiliar, but for the opposite reason, that Shakespeare uses in their Elizabethan and unfamiliar sense a large number of words which seem so familiar that there is no incentive to look for them in the glossary. It is hoped that a glossary arranged as below will make it easy to see at a glance what words and phrases in any particular scene require elucidation. A number of phrases are glossed by what seems to be, in their context, the modern equivalent rather than by lexicographical glosses on the words which compose them.

Act First

SCENE I

line		line	
3	CRYSTAL, bright	123	STAND, withstand
10	HIS, its	126	AGAZ'D, astounded
39	HOLDETH THEE IN AWE, makes you hold her in awe	132	VAWARD, vanguard
50	NOURISH, nurse	159	SUPPLY, reinforcement
88	INTERMISSIVE, at intervals	177	CHIEFEST STERN, helm

SCENE II

line		line	
7	OTHERWHILES, at times	121	MEAN, moderation
41	GIMMORS, joints		

SCENE III

line		line	
2	CONVEYANCE, trickery	30	PEEL'D, tonsured
13	WARRANTIZE, guarantee	31	PRODITOR, traitor

Act I Sc. iii—*continued*

line
37 CANVASS, toss, as in a blanket
42 BEARING-CLOTH, christening-robe
53 WINCHESTER GOOSE, one suffering from venereal disease (the stews at Southwark were in the see of Winchester)

line
61 DISTRAIN'D, annexed
63 MOTIONS, causes
81 BREAK OUR MINDS AT LARGE, say plainly what we think
84 CLUBS, the call to the prentices to break up a riot

SCENE IV

8 ESPIALS, spies
15 'GAINST IT, aimed at it
33 PILL'D, cheap (*lit.* 'stripped')
53 SHOT, gunners
54 MINUTE WHILE, minute's space

54 LINSTOCK, stick with 'match'
65 BATTERY, attack
107 PUZZEL, harlot
    DOLPHIN, *i.e.* dauphin

SCENE V

5 CONJURE, exorcise

12 HIGH-MINDED, arrogant

Act Second

SCENE I

3 APPARENT, manifest
4 COURT OF GUARD, guardroom
11 SECURE, free of care

63 QUARTERS, posts
77 PLATFORMS, plans

SCENE II

28 TRULL, harlot

60 MEAN, intend

SCENE III

line
10 CENSURE OF, judgment on
23 WRITHLED, wrinkled
27 SORT, choose
35 TRAINED, enticed

line
36 SHADOW, image
73 MISCONSTER, misconstrue
79 CATES, delicacies

SCENE IV

14 BEAR HIM, carry himself
17 NICE, subtle
   QUILLETS, quibbles (*quidlibet*)
53 OPINION, reputation
71 HIS, its
76 FASHION, behaviour
85 CRESTLESS, without coat of arms
86 BEARS HIM, conducts himself
   ON, according to
93 EXEMPT, excluded

93 GENTRY, 'Debrett' or 'The Social Register'
96 ATTACHED, arrested
   ATTAINTED, convicted
100 PARTAKER, supporter
102 APPREHENSION, notion
115 BRAV'D, flouted
123 UPON THY PARTY, as your partisan

SCENE V

5 PURSUIVANTS, heralds
9 EXIGENT, extremity
16 WITTING, knowing
25 SEQUESTRATION, being cut off
30 ENLARGEMENT, setting free
37 I MAY, *i.e.* that I may
40 KINDLY, as to a relation

59 DISCOVER, explain
70 MOV'D, *i.e.* that moved
95 WARRANT, indicate
121 SEE HIS BURIAL BETTER, see that the burial is better
128 BLOOD, rank

Act Third

SCENE I

10 PREFERR'D, brought forward
20 DEGREE, rank
47 KEEPS, lodges

48 PATRONAGE, authorise
55 OFFICE, duty
93 UNACCUSTOM'D, lawless

Act III   Sc. i—*continued*

line		line	
99	INKHORN MATE, scribbler	131	HATH, has received
103	PITCH A FIELD, engage in battle		GIRD, rebuke
110	PREFER, advocate	169	REGUERDON, reward

SCENE II

2	POLICY, strategy	44	DARNEL, weeds
10	MEAN, method	123	BRAVES, taunts
19	SECURE, carefree		CHARLES HIS GLEEKS, Charles's jibes
20	PRACTISANTS, accomplices		
25	TO, compared to	124	AMORT, downcast
	WHICH, by which	134	COUCHED, levelled

SCENE III

1	DISMAY, be dismayed	10	DIFFIDENCE, distrust
3	CARE, grieving	24	EXTIRPED, uprooted
10	CUNNING, skill		

SCENE IV

23	REGUERDON'D, rewarded	39	PRESENT, immediate
32	PATRONAGE, 'back'		

Act Fourth

SCENE I

38	MOST EXTREMES, last extremity	103	GLOSS, disguise
71	PREVENTED, anticipated	167	DIGEST, work off
102	QUAINT CONCEIT, elaborate invention		

SCENE II

line
12 EVEN, level
13 AIR-BRAVING, challenging the winds of heaven
26 APPARENT SPOIL, visible destruction
29 RIVE, discharge
34 DUE, endue

line
43 PERUSE, examine
45 PARK'D, enclosed
PALE, palisade
48 IN BLOOD, in condition
49 RASCAL, a deer out of condition
50 MOODY, dangerous

SCENE III

10 SUPPLY, reinforcements
25 CORNETS, squadrons

33 LONG OF, in consequence of

SCENE IV

5 BUCKLED, grappled

19 IN ADVANTAGE, in a strong position

SCENE V

22 YOUR REGARD, regard for yourself

SCENE VI

3 FRANCE HIS, France's
9 DATE, limit

35 MICKLE, great

SCENE VII

9 GUARDANT, guard
10 TENDERING MY RUIN, watching over my fall

21 LITHER, yielding
35 WOOD, mad
41 GIGLOT, wanton

Act Fifth

SCENE I

SCENE III

SCENE IV

SCENE V